Jamie,

Here's to old [...]

& many more years of

positive _Momentum_ !

PRAISE FOR RELATIONSHIP MOMENTUM

"Brian's ideas and principles on building your brand and moving your ideas forward are important for any successful entrepreneur."

— Daymond John
Founder of FUBU and star of ABC's *Shark Tank*

"I would recommend this book to anyone looking to create movement for their ideas or their endeavors."

— Brian Moran
Author of *The 12 Week Year*

"Mr. Church asks an important question: What makes certain businesses successful and others fail? While it appears on the surface that there is no easy answer based on conventional wisdom, Brian shares with us the valuable insights he has gained through his many dynamic business ventures, and points out that the key to a business's success is in fact having the ability to discern the intangible...discern the environment that surrounds us, the relationships, the momentum and energy of interaction with others that we can harness and amplify. To help the reader understand the concept and components within *Relationship Momentum* and be able to actually apply it to one's own business, Mr. Church breaks down the elements into discreet – and most importantly, modifiable

– factors in a mathematical formula, which appeals to me greatly as an ophthalmic researcher and cataract and LASIK surgeon who is committed to precision, accuracy, principles and their application. *Relationship Momentum* is a must read for all who want to find the key to unlock the door for the ultimate business success and satisfaction of human endeavors."

— **Dr. Ming Wang**
CEO of Wang Institute, Harvard, MIT (MD), PhD Laser Physics

"Brian will get you in the Success Red Zone with his powerful new book, *Relationship Momentum*. I understand the challenges from start-up to stardom. With *Relationship Momentum*, the distance between dream and reality will be a lot shorter. Thanks Brian for showing us the path."

— **Roe Frazer**
CEO, Cicayda, llc.

"Hard skills, what we know, account for only a small portion of success in business or in life. Soft skills are far more important. And there is no soft skill more important than getting along with other people. As long as you can create and maintain long-term relationships, you will never be out of business. Knowing your product or knowing your idea will only get you started toward your goal. Relating to others and being adept at creating relationships will keep you moving. It will separate you from the pack. Nobody knows that better than Brian Church. The racks are full of books telling us to form meaningful relationships. *Relationship Momentum* is one of the few books, if not the only book, telling us how to do it."

— **Don Connelly**
Nationally Renowned Speaker, Motivator, and Educator

"I strongly recommend this book for human studies beyond ordinary reading for pleasure and as a way of helping our world and individuals to successful living. I believe the best contribution anyone can make to improve our world is to pass unto others whatever knowledge that has been revealed to help others succeed.

This is what Brian Church has done and I am not surprised at that because of my personal relationship with him and others in Adassa-Adumori Foundation who have helped to build Emure Kingdom of Ekiti State, Nigeria. Enjoy reading this wonderful exposition to knowledge on the pathway to a successful life."

— His Royal Majesty, King Emmanuel Adebayo,
The Ellemure of Emure Kingdom, Africa

"I first met Brian in 2006 at a fund-raising event for under privileged children. I remember my first impression of Brian. I thought to myself, 'this guy is going somewhere.' And, as the years have evidenced, he has. Brian is good at his craft, very good. He is assisting my start-up company, Ebars, and me in *Relationship Momentum*. I know it's a major key to our future success. I'm confident in the wisdom found in this book. Brian's work of Art and Science will open your eyes as it has mine onto one of the best-kept and most mysterious secrets to success."

— Dave Dalton
President and Founder of Ebars

"As a classic Liberal Arts (Relationship-Driven) business-person, I feared my eyes would glaze over with the introduction of physics properties in the text. I quickly realized though, that the physical principles were simply a new way of presenting the fundamental properties of mutually beneficial relationships. I'm not sure if Brian Church's work is a very sophisticated thesis boiled down into a very simple and effective message or if it is a very simple and effective message presented in such a way as to appeal to, and motivate, a highly sophisticated audience. Either way, this is solid, thought provoking reading! This book provides a focused lens through which I can better assess my approach to international projects and the key relationships on which they depend; and the dynamics for progress – or lack thereof."

— Pat McRae
Former US Diplomat

"Brian Church has given us a gift in his new book *Relationship Momentum*. By taking a revolutionary approach by combining science, math, art and relationships, Brian has created a new lens for seeing, understanding, and realizing the potential of our ideas. After reading this book, you will never view Relationships in the same way again."

— Howard Ragsdale
President and CEO, Arbor Healthcare

"As one who has earned his PhD in physics, I have always been a bit leery of business professionals who argue for parallels between physics principles and their industries. Often their lack of understanding results in their attempted use of physics concepts to range from the clumsy to the misleading. However, Brian Church's book is a notable exception. Not only does he relate physics concepts reliably, but his parallels are extremely insightful. I have consulted in various industries over the past few decades, and his insights on organizational dynamics are some of the freshest and most applicable I have encountered."

— Brian Miller
BS Physics-MIT, PhD Physics-Duke, Business Consultant

"A must read! Brian answers the how and why of maximizing your biggest asset — your relationships."

— Nick Pagano
Author of *Abnormal Journey*

"Brian presents the unique and fascinating connection between the laws of motion and physics with the art and science of business relationships, an Entrepreneur's exploration of the convergence of science and success!"

— Charles Bone
Chairman, Founder of Bone McAllester Norton

"The correlation of Relationships and Momentum is hard to describe because it is hard to quantify. Brian has done an amazing job taking the principles he's learned and turning them into a blue print. If it weren't for Brian and his formula, I would not be doing what I am doing today."

— Joe Brannon
Co-Founder of textLIVING

"Brian Church has managed to transform an ancient scientific principal into a fresh concept for today's business professional. I predict his readers will be moved, like I was, from building relationships instinctively to intentionally."

— Pat Baldridge
President, Charlotte Christian Chamber of Commerce

"Brian is a thoughtful leader who continually challenged me to take personal responsibility, confront reality, and produce experiences that organizations and people care deeply about. The truth is our success cannot be achieved in a vacuum. Relationships are an essential part of the equation. In *Relationship Momentum*, Brian unpacks immutable laws for making ideas happen in and through others."

— Rob Harvey
Social Entrepreneur and Chairman of Good Neighbor Foundation

"Brian brilliantly intertwines high-touch concepts like physics with digestible anecdotes and personal stories, giving both the mainstream and academic reader takeaways that will last a lifetime. Grounded in science and confirmed through years of personal application, *Relationship Momentum* provides the tools and principles necessary for each of us to see our personal 'brand' flourish and our influence increase."

— David Litwin
CEO Pure Fusion Media, Inc. and author of *Parables & Parrallels*

RELATIONSHIP MOMENTUM

RELATIONSHIP MOMENTUM

The Secret to Making Ideas Move!

BRIAN T. CHURCH

DUNHAM
books

For Kimberly

CONTENTS

FOREWORD

I wish I had read this book thirty years ago. You have just begun to read a book that has the potential to make things move in your business and career. Innovators know that if we are not able to create and sustain forward momentum, then we will (in effect) slide backwards. Consequently, those who are able to identify and manage the elements of positive and negative momentum in their careers, businesses, and personal lives are the ones on their way to success. In *Relationship Momentum* Brian Church has shown us how to do that, and he articulates it brilliantly. He is introducing a solution that is relevant in today's environment, easy to understand, and completely reproducible.

I have had the pleasure of knowing Brian for nearly his entire life. Being dear friends and business partners with his father for many years, I saw Brian grow from boy to young man and to the business leader he is today. He inherited his father's entrepreneurial drive and has developed an uncanny talent for distilling out essential ingredients of his success and the successes of others. In *Relationship Momentum* he explains them in concepts that are easy to understand and hard to deny. Even if you are stuck, stagnant, or dead in the water, the concepts in this book can help you create movement.

As I read an early draft, I was immediately struck by the fact that Brian had found a way to clearly convey some of the principles that had helped me build successful businesses multiple times throughout my life. It would have never occurred to me (or anyone else) to explain business success in terms of Sir Isaac Newton's Three Laws of Motion. However, after reading *Relationship Momentum,* it is now hard to think the dynamics of my own success or failures without a mental image of Newton smiling in approval or shaking his head in dismay.

My best example of the Relationship Momentum concept is when I took on the challenge of bringing an NBA franchise to Charlotte, NC. I needed to ensure that I was bringing a valuable Brand position to the fans. I needed to gather, cultivate and foster a tremendous base of Ambassadors through the value we brought to the region. And I needed to have a strategic plan that would help to maximize and maintain the increasing Momentum. The net effect was that everything we did was magnified and multiplied because of these principles. Even after I achieved that goal, I made sure the organization maintained its Relationship Momentum by staying focused on nurturing and expanding relationships. Strong Ambassadors were essential to the Hornets throughout my time as owner. Concepts that Brian identifies as Value, Brand, and Ambassador Equities correlate with the essential ingredients of our accomplishments. We reached the pinnacle of success, leading the NBA in attendance for nine straight seasons despite being in its smallest market.

I have always believed that I was empowered by my relationship with God, the strengths of my personal relationships (friends and family), and by knowing and staying true to what I wanted to accomplish. Every time I began to head off in the wrong direction, it was always because these areas had become out of sync and were not pulling in the same direction. I wish I had these lessons many years ago. It would have given me a framework, enabling me to more consistently and more efficiently focus my attention on things that really matter — things that contribute to Relationship Momentum in all aspects of my life.

Relationship Momentum will absolutely get you focused on the highly efficient and highly effective pathway to greater success in your endeavors. If you want to see your ideas progress, you must find a formula for your relationships to move. I thoroughly enjoyed this book and I know you will too.

– George Shinn
Horatio Alger Award Winner and Founder of the Charlotte Hornets

INTRODUCTION

The Reader's Path

> *"It's a new dawn, it's a new day, it's a new life for me . . .*
> *and I'm feeling good!"*
> — Nina Simone

There I was, sitting in the lobby of one of the largest footwear companies in the world. My team was with me — people with resumes that would make a Fortune 100 company envious. In my bag was one of the most robust and disruptive pieces of new technology that had come along in years. The objective was to enter into a collaborative effort to infuse this technology into the footwear company's products and then release it to the industry at large. The indications of interest were high. We made it to the front door of a successful product launch . . . only to have it slammed in our face. The loss was a crushing blow to our new company. We approached a few other smaller players with the technology but never found any real traction. We lost our fervor and belief in the new product and eventually abandoned it for "the next great idea."

I reflected on this for years, wondering what could have been done differently to change the outcome. As it turned out, there was a fundamental breakdown with one of our key relationships nearly six months prior to our big meeting at the company's home office. The issue certainly could have been avoided and it has helped to inspire some of the concepts in this book.

I have similar stories to this one. I have been blessed with the opportunity to spend time in myriad industries. I have worked with corporations, advisers, entrepreneurs, and inventors. I have had my fair share of successes, but far too many losses, abandoned dreams, and setbacks. As I tried my best to steward my defeats, I began to notice a common theme.

At the center of every success you will find a pivotal relationship. Conversely, you can trace the cause of most failures to a relationship vacuum or breakdown.

Behind every great company or product, you will find elements that contribute to positive Momentum. Behind every failed venture, there is always the presence of stagnation.

Throughout my years in the global marketplace, one thing has consistently astounded me. Individuals experiencing expansion or contraction, success or failure in their endeavors, usually do not know why. Many attribute their success or failure to outside forces. In other words, success or failure (more likely failure) is something that has *"happened to them"* rather than something that was driven by them. Others try to explain their career direction in terms of factors unrelated to their advancement or decline.

This book is about my search to understand the art and science of why some ideas progress and some dissipate; why some people advance in their careers with sustained movement, while others seem to be swimming upstream, working hard but continually falling back. The search was to find a cause-and-effect answer, a formula rather, that would provide me with a clear path on which ideas, ideals, and careers could move.

I have discovered that the answer has little to do with natural ability, but rather encompasses a few key components executed with diligence and audacity. I want the reader to understand that achieving their personal and professional objectives is not based solely on personality types, the business environment, or even unique giftings. On the contrary, the eventual success or failure of their ideas will hinge primarily upon their ability to create and manage this one concept. My findings? The secret to making your ideas move and the key element behind all product, project, or purpose-driven growth is what I call Relationship Momentum.™

I am not a physicist or an authority on Newton's Laws of Motion. I'm just an entrepreneur who has a calling to help people with their God-given ideas. I have been searching for sensible answers to some simple questions —why some initiatives succeed and others fail. Though at times I may appeal to scientific principles and express dependent relations in terms of mathematical formulas, trust me — if the components I introduce in these pages were not practical and simple to implement, I would not have been a part of the project. I'm not interested in theories, formulas or equations unless they lead directly to results.

I was fortunate enough to recruit a team of physicists, entrepreneurs, professors, and friends who committed to help me on this project. Our goal was to take historical evidence, along with my personal wins and losses, in order to correlate the science of movement with the art of relationship building. We then set out to clearly define and test the equation for Relationship Momentum and to make it transferrable to all. We identified three spheres of Relationship Momentum — personal, spiritual, and vocational — those which the concepts of this book can affect. This particular manuscript deals mostly with the vocational realm.

I suggest that you read this book much like I wrote it. The chapters are made up of bite-size meditations that can each stand alone to induce thought. They are a collection of truths, laws, and ideas that the team or I have acquired along the way. I did not write the chapters of the book in sequential order. Nevertheless, the arrangement of the chapters was intentional. They provide a blueprint for applying the formula of Relationship Momentum.

The progression of the book is simple. I have arranged the chapters into three sections that coincide with the Relationship Momentum Equation:

$$Rm=E^3V_s$$

Rm — The first section, denoted by the symbol for Relationship Momentum, chronicles the evolution of the ideas in this book and the supporting evidence as to why relationships, Momentum, and the other supporting elements are essential for your growth.

E^3 — This symbol represents the Three Equities: Brand, Value, and Ambassador. This is the meat of the book. Here I explain the Three Equities as a substitute for Mass, while providing several new concepts and applications of how to maximize each of them.

V_s — This symbol represents Strategic Velocity. We will examine the importance of Velocity, but more importantly the strategic nature of how you identify, grow, and then sustain Relationship Momentum.

The purpose of the book is to provide you with a formula that you can test against any idea or endeavor during its life cycle (beginning, middle, or end). The chapters are designed to set the stage, deliver the idea, support its findings, and then show you how to use and sustain them.

This project was written for everyone who has ever had an idea or an agenda. A paper napkin sketch or musing that they dreamed of sharing with the world. A product, project, or purpose that they wanted to propel. Like many, I have read scores of books that promised to help me turn the corner of success. Most left me searching for answers to implied questions or specific methods of action. I was looking for answers that were grounded in the real world; perhaps you are too. This book contains a different approach. People are not accustomed to thinking about success in the context of Sir Isaac Newton's Laws of Motion. However, I am confident that after a few chapters, you will be evaluating everything around you in terms of concepts like Momentum, Drag, and even Net Velocity.

I invite you to think through these concepts with me. At some point along the way you may have an epiphany as I did — that "Ah Ha!" moment in which you begin to see Relationship Momentum as the catalyst and the answer for helping your ideas and initiatives move.

— **Brian Church**

PART I

Rm

A New Concept

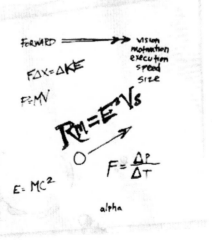

1

THE UNDERLYING
CONSTANT OF SUCCESS

*"Truth is ever to be found in the simplicity, and not in
the multiplicity and confusion of things."*

— Sir Isaac Newton

The physical universe operates by a set of constants — laws that do
not change with time, trends, or public opinion. They are the true
reasons things work the way they do, irrespective of commonly held
beliefs, imagined formulas, or magic potions.

Sir Isaac Newton did not create Gravity, nor did he discover it. In
1666, the year of Newton's apple-tree revelation, everyone knew that
when an apple detached from its tree, it fell straight down to the earth.
There were, however, plenty of ideas about why such things happened.
Hyper-spiritualists might have said that angels picked the apples and
threw them down to the ground. Others probably said that an apple
falls *just because it does*, and that is all anyone needs to know. Any

further investigation was a waste of time. Aristotle would have said the apple falls because of its natural place in the universe — that is, heavy objects like rocks "wanted" to be at rest on the earth and that light objects like smoke "wanted" to be at rest in the sky. This was an interesting idea, but it was not very useful, because it only described *what* had happened. It could not predict what the object would do next, or explain *why* they "wanted" to do it.

Isaac Newton simply broke down the falling-apple process and explained precisely why it happens the way it does. The result eventually became Newton's Law of Universal Gravitation and his three Laws of Motion. Perhaps "simply" is not the best word to describe what Newton did because he had to invent the mathematics of calculus to prove his theory. A better word might be "clearly." Newton so *clearly* explained the dynamics of Gravity and Motion that he demystified the phenomena and revealed it to be something very predictable. In fact, the true test of Newton's theory was its ability to accurately predict planetary movements.

I spent many years in the business of innovating, selling, and recruiting — not without some degree of success. I have been fortunate enough to become a respected business owner, business Ambassador and human capital specialist. I have personally contributed to the successful launch of numerous new products and companies. I have been blessed enough to consult for corporations, CEOs, pastors, managers, and even a king, with regards to relationships and Momentum. I have also had more than my fair share of failures. Always eager to improve, I read all the books, attended the seminars, and experimented with numerous ideas — all promising to be the key to phenomenal success. I knew that all those ideas (at least the ones that made any sense) revolved around relationships. However, turning relationships into real success was a lot like trying to understand apples falling out of the Newton's tree. I would read a biography about a top executive and their journey to the zenith of their respective industry, but I could not clearly break down the process that made it all happen.

Of course, there is no shortage of theories about why people succeed. But the only Value of the theories I explored was in the description of one person's individual path to achievement, what one person had done and far less predictive of what others might do. In other words, so and so seemed to have worked for a great CEO and he was cited as the reason for his success. However, the same principle proved ineffective for me. Eventually, I became a bit cynical about all the advice, feeling that those proposing all the theories of success had not really gotten to the bottom of it. Perhaps the truth was that those who succeeded did so simply because they had the gift, and those without that gift were simply wasting their time. In other words, some apples fall to the ground just because they do, and that's all we can really know about it.

When Sir Isaac Newton was asked about how he had made his remarkable discoveries, he is reported to have said, "By thinking about it all the time." I'm no Isaac Newton, but I have been thinking about the correlation between success and relationships for a while now. I have seen something in the great scientist that directly applies to everything I have ever tried to do. Newton's three Laws of Motion (inertia, applied force, and corresponding reactions) seemed to be that underlying component to all the theories and stories about the impact of success. The more I thought about it, applied it to previous experiences, and tested it in new ventures, the more I came to realize that the Momentum of Relationships was the determining factor in the success or failure of every salesperson, business leader, or social change agent. No matter what you are trying to measure — business ventures, marriages, fund raising, or any other pursuit — the dynamic of Momentum as it relates to your relationships will be the surest predictor of its relative success or failure.

ISAAC NEWTON AND OCKHAM'S RAZOR

Ockham's razor is a principle of scientific research (also known as *lex parsimoniae* or the Law of Parsimony) that stipulates the following: "if two theories equally explain and predict observable phenomena, then the simpler of the two is usually the true cause." The word "Ockham" comes from the philosophy of William of Ockham (*c.* 1285–1349), and "razor" refers to the process of shaving off the excess. Isaac Newton wrote, "We are to admit no more causes of natural things than such as are both true and sufficient to explain their appearances." Note that it is not just the simplest answer but the simplest answer *that works.*

Efforts to explain Gravity on the basis of angels or objects that "want" to behave in certain ways were unscientific; since they could not predict events, they could not be tested, proven, or disproven. Newton's Universal Law of Gravitation was not the first theory put forth to predict the motion of planets. Two hundred years earlier, planetary movements were predicted by unimaginably complex calculations. They were so complex because they were based on a faulty premise — that the sun and stars revolved around the earth. For that same reason, they were less than precise in their predictions.

Newton predicted the motion of planets with unprecedented accuracy that was limited only by the precision of measuring instruments (telescopes). No one suggests that his calculus was simple, but his theory of Universal Gravitation and his three Laws of Motion were elegant in their simplicity. First realizing this, Newton must have jumped to his feet and shouted, "AH HA! THAT'S IT!"

Regarding principles of success in business, the "ah ha" for me came with the concept of Relationship Momentum. All the ideas and anecdotes about the sure-fire keys to success began to look as artificially complex as a medieval planetary calculator or as speculative as theories about objects "wanting" to be on the ground or in the air.

Thinking about moving from where I am to where I want to be in my career, about the ability to overcome obstacles and break through barriers, I realized that there is no concept more basic than Momentum — the product of Velocity and Mass. That's not to suggest that it is simple and easy to manage relationships that produce strategically directed Momentum. Often it is not. However, the fundamental concept upon which every other idea rests is elegant, sound, and (by the shaving of Ockham's razor) simple.

2
THE RELATIONSHIP DECONSTRUCTED

"Human relationships always help us to carry on because they always presuppose further developments, a future — and also because we live our lives as if our only task was precisely to have relationships with other people."

— Albert Camus

Deep within the psyche of every human is an inherent need for love, for peer esteem, and for personal accomplishment. All of the aforementioned are psychological needs that are dependent upon relationships. When addressing the topic of basic human needs, eventually the conversation turns to psychologist Abraham Maslow (1905-1970). Maslow, a Russian Jewish immigrant, first published his theory on the hierarchy of human needs in a 1943 paper entitled *The Theory of Human Motivation*, in which he identified five ascending levels of basic human needs.

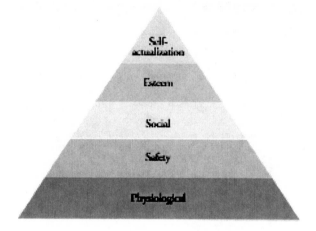

1. PHYSIOLOGICAL NEEDS such as oxygen, water, food, and sleep.
2. SAFETY AND SECURITY NEEDS that include a safe and stable environment, protection, job, and retirement security.
3. SOCIAL NEEDS which ranges from being loved to being accepted as a part of a group.
4. THE NEED FOR ESTEEM. In its lower form, esteem includes respect from others, status, fame, recognition, etc. In its higher form, esteem means self-respect, confidence, and personal achievement.
5. SELF-ACTUALIZATION is the need for meaningful accomplishment at one's highest potential, where experiences and core competencies are put to maximum use.

Maslow noticed that these needs were generally fulfilled sequentially. Self-esteem (level 4) is not a pressing concern if you are starving (level 2), and you quickly forget about food (level 2) if you can't breathe (level 1), and so on- thus the term "hierarchy of needs." Certainly, one can achieve belonging, esteem, and meaningful accomplishment without being physiologically or monetarily secure. However, the general tendency is that the most basic need is the most pressing need.

SURRENDERING TO HUMAN ENGINEERING

Every human is engineered to long for community, insomuch that every form of success or failure derives its meaning and significance from relationships. The measure of our relationships is not only the formula for personal Momentum, but a source by which we define meaning and purpose for our lives. The American mystique, however, is characterized by rugged individualism — the cowboy riding the range, completely self-sufficient without care or concern for what others think. That image suggests that all those needs for love, for esteem, and for success (Maslow's levels three, four, and five) are all self-contained — that is, those needs are met without dependence on anyone outside of one's self. Whenever you hear someone say that they don't care what anyone else thinks, it is often a sign that they actually care more deeply than the average person. But having failed to gain the love and acceptance or the esteem among peers, family, and friends, some have simply tried to rewrite Maslow. In other words, they attempt to fill the higher level needs apart from relationships. In terms of progress toward their highest goals, they try to build Momentum without relationships.

According to a recent *New York Times* study, twenty-five percent of Americans say that they feel alone. So, is it any wonder why so many of our initiatives fail? This is not intended to be a touchy-feely book. I do, however, feel the need to challenge you to think about the epicenter of every success or failure up to this point. It can all be traced back to relationships.

How many people do you know who have lived for years with frustration over this one point? They feel endowed with the ideas and talents that should propel them to the top of their fields or industries. Yet, they see people who (in their opinion) are less skilled, less gifted, and less dedicated, pass them by on the way to success, esteem, and accomplishment.

Maybe you are one of those people and just never had the courage to admit the jealousy of others' success. As time goes on and if the lack of progress relative to others prevails, you may find yourself growing more and more frustrated at what seems to be the charmed life of others. When carried to its logical ends, that frustration may turn into resentment because you feel passed over; giving rise to suspicion about favoritism, cheating, or conspiracies, or eventually creating unrealistic self-appraisals (irrational delusions of grandeur that no one else appreciates). At this point, the focus begins to turn more inward and non-relational. With diminishing Relationship Momentum, the chances of success diminish as well. And so begins a downward spiral.

This is, of course, advancing quickly to the extreme conclusion. However, just as the formula for success is universally applicable, the seeds of this inward progression lie dormant in every person. No doubt, you have seen this in one degree or another in those working under you, those on your level, or (heaven help you) in those who are your superiors. Nothing is more bizarre than working under someone with diminishing Relationship Momentum. If that is your situation, be careful not to let the same seeds begin to take root within you.

Are you the one sitting at the back of the room, looking around at your peers and wondering why you are not farther ahead? Maybe you have advanced in a manner that has impressed others, but you know deep down that there is something missing. You may not have used the term "self-actualization," but you long for that place where your gifts and core competencies are put to their highest and most efficient use. In the coming pages, I share some formulas that have the potential to kick your idea and/ or career into another gear. However, you may have to change the way you think about your current and future relationships. The tendency is to think that personal success and personal performance is a "self thing," when, in fact, it is a "relationship thing."

The first step into that new way of thinking is to take inventory of your current relationships, what is working, and what may be lacking. The coming pages will help you evaluate those relationships, not just in terms of benefit to you, but also in terms of your contribution to the success of others. Ask yourself, what kind of Momentum are your relationships creating for you at the present? Conversely, are you the kind of friend and associate that is creating Momentum for the relationships around you?

3
RELATIONSHIPS[3]

"The meeting of two personalities is like the contact of two chemical substances: if there is any reaction, both are transformed."
— C.G. Jung

The secret to developing great relationships is the ability to identify the nature of the relationship and the type of benefit each party derives from it. If you go into a relationship without a clear and mutual understanding of the type of relationship and the desired benefit, most likely no one in that relationship is going to be completely satisfied.

A girl is looking for love and determined to get it. A guy is looking for sex and is equally determined. One of them, if not both, is going to be very disappointed.

Two acquaintances go out for coffee after a social gathering. One is looking for friendship, the other for the opportunity to give a sales pitch. Here, there are two different motivations: one seeking friendship (an emotional relationship) and the other seeking a sale (a business relationship). Once again, someone, if not everyone, is going to be disappointed.

In the example above, the salesman was masquerading as someone looking for friendship. But in *his* mind, selling his product or business would indeed benefit his new acquaintance — at least that's what his sales manager taught him to believe. Business relationships can indeed be beneficial to both. The problem, however, was that the individuals did not share a mutual understanding of why they were getting together for coffee. Often the most intensely negative feelings about sales techniques are reserved for people who try to initiate friendships with hidden agendas.

You can create these scenarios all day long. You can also think back to some unproductive business partnerships (both informal and formal) and view them in terms of the type of relationship and the expectations placed upon it. Were all parties in for the same reasons and with the same objectives in mind? In most cases, they were not. Understanding the dynamics of Relationship Momentum on the front end will save a lot of time, money, and emotional turmoil on the backend.

I like the way Anthony Robbins put it when he said, "The only way a relationship will last is if you see that relationship as a place you go to give and not a place that you go to take." I would add that the only way relationships will last is if *both parties* mutually benefit, that is, if the relationship satisfies the needs of both parties. Productive relationships that create Momentum in your life have both a give and a take element.

I simply do not have room in my life for one-way relationships. That doesn't mean I am not interested in building friendships or charitable relationships. If I am helping someone pro bono, mentoring a recent college grad, or reading to at-risk youth, I get tremendous benefit out of that — usually more than I give. As examined in the prior chapter, we are given certain gifts and created with certain needs. My charitable work is done with no expectation of a financial return, but the emotional return is priceless. I feel needed. I feel selfless. I feel joy. All of that comes from making a difference in another person's life without any expectation of reciprocity. I am fulfilling one of the hardwired needs instilled in us by the Great Engineer.

THERE ARE THREE FORMS OF RELATIONSHIPS

Emotional — Relationships that fulfill our need for community and companionship.

Emotional Relationships usually form naturally as they draw upon common interests, values, backgrounds, or social styles. They form strong bonds that create the most loyal of alliances. That much you already know. The true art of emotional relationships is the ability to shorten the timeline to building these types of partnerships, creating long-lasting friendships quickly by building upon honesty, common purpose, and mutual benefit.

Economic — Relationships that produce some type of monetary exchange or enterprise Value. To put it another way, these are monetized relationships. However, many of these relationships are short-lived unless those involved figured out how to manage the accounts — that is, to maintain the balance of Value that each person or business gains from that relationship. In a future chapter on Ambassador Equity, I will talk about managing, maintaining, and multiplying the Value you bring to a business relationship. Without a continually expanding sense of Value, business relationships grow old and stale. Like any other relationship, people on both ends begin to take those mutual benefits for granted. Energy and enthusiasm drain from service, support, performance, and compensation. Short-lived relationships create little positive Momentum. In some cases, the net result is negative Momentum (Drag) toward your strategic objective.

Tactical — Relationships that fulfill a specific and limited purpose. They produce a transactional response to an immediate need and are measured by immediate results. One person or entity needs something and another person or entity delivers. For example, someone is hired as a marketing consultant for a financial advisory firm. The consultant then hires telemarketers to set appointments that benefit all parties involved. The relationship to the employing client and the marketing consultant was most likely economic and perhaps even emotional in nature. The relationship between the employing client and the telemarketing firm is merely tactical. The service is beneficial, yet only tactical in nature.

The Difference

Tactical relationships are short-term arrangements focused on fixing defined problems. More strategic relationships like those based on economics or emotions are usually long term; they are goal oriented, and deal with making decisions that direct your life toward those objectives.

MANAGING SPHERES OF RELATIONSHIPS

The practical application to all this is learning how to manage spheres of relationships. Because we get sick, pay taxes, and grow grass, I have tactical relationships with doctors, accountants, and lawn-care professionals. Momentum in these tactical relationships is measured through the treatment of the customer. If I neglect to build relationships with these people or treat them badly, my life may become unbearably chaotic.

Because I am in hot pursuit of business and career goals, I have a clearly defined and growing group of mutually beneficial relationships. This is a concept we will discuss in depth later. I call this my Embassy. Though we enjoy one another as friends who play golf, attend church, and participate together in community service initiatives, the serious business of our relationship is to help one another reach our highest personal and career potential. Long-term relationships impact my life in many ways, and maintaining those relationships is of the highest priority.

Then there are relationships that are forever — family and a few individuals. These are the relationships that I can never give up on, irrespective of mutual benefit. I am committed to them no matter what.

There is, of course, some overlap in the spheres. Some tactical relationships become business partners. Some family members, like my father, have been essential to my career success. The point is that I am very clear about the purpose and priority of relationships and very intentional about maintaining them.

ON-PURPOSE RELATIONSHIPS

It is quite amazing to me how people go to such great lengths to initiate and maintain relationships without a clear idea about the type or purpose. Relationships are serious business and are the mortar for the proverbial bricks of life. They should be defined, stewarded, and in some cases, measured for their validity, utility, and productivity.

This will probably sound very mechanical to some readers, as if I am treating people like tools or products. That is, in fact, the very opposite of how I feel. I put my relationships with people at the very top of my priority list, and I value those people for who they are, not simply for what they can do for me. However, my desire is for meaningful, long-lasting relationships in which we mutually challenge and propel one another to our highest potential as husbands, wives, fathers, mothers, citizens, colleagues, and business persons. I would rather have a dozen of those than a hundred superficial relationships that are of little benefit to others — or to me.

Let's be honest. Some of us have a greater relationship capacity than others, but everyone has a limit to the number of people they can know on a deep level. Because people take a casual approach to relationships, they have essentially wasted their emotional investments in them without serious thought to the purpose or benefit. The unfortunate result is that some people have not a single relationship that is producing positive Momentum toward their strategic objectives. As a result the products, projects and purposes in their lives limp along, with neither the Velocity to achieve their goals, nor the Force to overcome obstacles in their way.

4
ORGANIZATIONAL PHYSICS

"Success requires first expending ten units of effort to produce one unit of results. Your Momentum will then produce ten units of results with each unit of effort."
— Charles J. Givens

The number one rule in battle is to never give up ground that has already been taken. You end up fighting twice for the same victory. How many people do that in their daily lives with their endeavors? I once sat in a room with a pastor and a very close friend of mine who happened to be a serial inventor. The pastor said to that inventor, "You are like a long train of box cars, each one filled with valuable ideas. However, your engine and cargo never reach its final destination." My friend did not have an energy problem or an idea problem; he had a Momentum problem.

It was once said that "the road to failure is paved by good intentions." Think of all the great projects, ideas, and companies that are out there. Each one began with an idea. That unfortunate thing is that 99 out of 100 good ideas never become a reality. Many ideas fail due to what I call "the Emotional Cycle of Momentum."

Emotional Cycle of Momentum

Idea — Optimism — The Great Escape

Uninformed — Informed

Valley of Despair — Pessimism — Moment of Faith / Quit or Push Forward

RELATIONSHIP MOMENTUM

In the illustration above, an idea begins with great optimism — enthusiastic but uninformed optimism. The inventor begins to move that idea along but also begins to suspect that things may not be as easy as he had imagined (uninformed pessimism). He presses onward, only to discover that there are indeed formidable obstacles and more competition than he realized (informed pessimism). At this point, a majority of those 100 ideas evaporate. The inventor returns to the drawing board and waits for the next great idea to pursue. A small number of those original 100 ideas, perhaps even one in a thousand, become successful due to the effort of an individual who continues to press forward. One simply cannot short cut the fact that faith in the idea and a commitment to seeing it through must be present to survive the valley of despair. If the creator can press through to seeing the fruit of his labors (informed optimism), the dream becomes reality and Momentum can be clearly identified. Remember this: One of the myths of the Emotional Cycle of Momentum is that there is no Momentum present along the ride. It is often there; it's just harder to see.

We like to talk about the freedom and virtues associated with a fresh start. There are many benefits personally, vocationally, and spiritually to getting a clean slate, to pressing the reset button. Starting over can be refreshing, exhilarating, and full of excitement for the opportunity to get right what before always seemed to go wrong. However, repeatedly starting over is a bad habit that is both the effect and further cause of negative Momentum.

Think of it in spiritual terms. We love to talk about grace, forgiveness, and the ability to start over. Yes, that is an essential part of it. At the same time, the greatest spiritual, emotional, and even financial blessings are the result of long-term faithfulness to a single idea. Recurring cycles of failure, repentance, forgiveness, and starting over are like spinning wheels in the mud. Grace is not just the ability to start anew; it is the power to overcome the obstacles that have repeatedly stopped you. The bottom line is that we have to stop starting over.

DISCIPLINE, MILESTONES, AND SUSTAINED MOMENTUM

Jim Collins and Morten Hansen's latest book, *Great By Choice*, is the result of a nine-year research project aimed at answering one question: "Why do some companies thrive in uncertainty, even chaos, and others do not?" Collins and Hansen identified what they call "10x Companies." They write:

"We set out to find companies that started from a position of vulnerability, rose to become great companies with spectacular performance, and did so in unstable environments characterized by big forces, out of their control, fast moving, uncertain, and potentially harmful" (7).

Imagine walking from San Diego to Maine. Your goal is to march twenty miles per day, every day, regardless of the weather. You don't march farther even though you have ambition to achieve, and you don't do less because you are tired. A key characteristic of the 10x companies is that they identify what their 20-mile march is and stick to it with the rhythm of a metronome. As a co-founder of an intellectual property think tank, I have seen so many people kick, claw, and scratch their way to some milestone. At that point many lose their motivation, sit down, and admire their most recent accomplishment as they fall farther behind the attainment of their potential accomplishment. Fanatic discipline is necessary to create Momentum for an individual or a company. It is sustainable Momentum because the personal habits enable them to keep going with great regularity in the most difficult of circumstances.

STRATEGIC MOMENTUM

Once you identify Momentum, you must maximize it and sustain it. It would be hard to debate the undisputed need for Momentum in your initiatives. Momentum is movement in a consistent direction and is represented by the equation $P = MV$ which is: Momentum = Mass x Velocity.

In dealing with a product, project, or purpose, all movement has a relational component. Therefore we are not simply looking for movement in a consistent direction but strategic relational movement with a degree of urgency. What relationships do you currently have that will keep you from fighting for the same ground over and over? In the coming pages, we will discuss how to identify and then maximize your Motion through a formula that will clearly illustrate your blue print for conquering new territory. Stop starting over, and start becoming fanatical about your Momentum.

5
THE SCIENCE OF HOW

"The credit for advancing science has always been due to
individuals and never the age."
— Johann Wolfgang Van Goethe

People have always searched for answers to questions about why things work the way they do — why some people or products are a success and why others are not. Business success formulas are everywhere, but most are just speculation based on anecdotal evidence. For example, let's suppose that a fantastically successful business executive dresses in Italian suits and drives cars that none of his competitors can afford. On each suit and car, his personal crest is boldly displayed. Someone will eventually propose a formula for success like the one below:

Monogrammed Cars + Monogrammed Suits = Success
or
Monogram (Cars + Suits) = Success

Formulas for business success are notorious for majoring on correlations (two things happening at the same time), but not so much on testable cause-and-effect relationships. In the example above, no one knows if the cars and suits caused the success or if it was the other way around. Perhaps the relationship between the suits and success was merely coincidental, or possibly they were both caused by the same thing (tertiary causation), such as his $100 million trust fund.

After chasing so many formulas, with each claiming to be the secret to success, people get a little jaded. They're not interested in another business story; they want some ideas with concrete cause-and-effect relationships that are verifiable by repeated tests. In other words, they need a testable theorem, which is defined as a proposition proved by a chain of reasoning; a truth accepted by a chain of excepted truths.

Since it was proving to be quite difficult to get my ideas moving and even harder to keep them consistently moving in the right direction, Sir Isaac Newton's Laws of Motion got my attention. Developed in 1667, the simplest of Newton's mechanics was his definition of Momentum, which is connected to his Second Law of Motion.

Momentum (traditionally designated as P) is the Mass of an object (m) times its Velocity (v).

$$Momentum = Mass\ x\ Velocity$$
$$or$$
$$P = MV$$

That formula for Momentum sounded very similar to a business and personal growth formula for which I had been searching. What I needed was consistent movement toward my goals, as well as the Momentum to overcome obstacles. Could I apply Newtonian mechanics to business and personal relationships? Why not? Mathematics and statistics have been applied to product design, time management, and consumer behavior for years. Movement is movement, whether it is a boulder, a battleship, or a relationship.

The more I thought about it and evaluated my relationships in the context of Newton's classical mechanics, the more Relationship Momentum became a natural way of directing and evaluating what I was doing. At first, viewing personal interactions in terms of an equation seemed awkward, but eventually $P = MV$ became my natural way of thinking about relationships. As time went on, I continued plugging in other aspects of business development. Consequently, I began to think of Relationship Momentum (designated by the symbol "Rm") as the various types of capital or Equity multiplied by the rate at which plans or objectives are moving forward (Velocity). I then specifically identified Three Equities as Brand Equity (personal or company reputation and Ethos), Value Equity (the utility my product, project, or purpose produces), and Ambassador Equity (Osmosis (viral) growth through multiple beneficial relationships).

The total Equity is a product of these three factors, that is, *Total Equity = A x B x C*. Of course, if any of those variables are zero, so will be the product of all three. In other words, you can have a valuable product and fabulous networking connections, but a terrible Brand that diminishes the impact of the whole. I will explain in detail each of those Three Equities later on. For now, just think of a large truck and these Equities as baskets of rocks. The more Equity you accumulate in these three baskets, the greater Mass your truck will have and the greater Momentum potential.

So, instead of the scientific formula for Momentum — Momentum equals Mass times Velocity (P=MV) — my relationship formula evolved to be: Relationship Momentum (Rm) equals the accumulated weight of those Three Equities (E^3) times Velocity (V).

$$Rm = E^3 V$$

STRATEGIC VELOCITY

In Newton's Law of Motion, the impact of Velocity and Force are referred to as "Net Velocity" and "Net Force." An object could have Forces being applied to it in several directions — 1,000 pounds per second squared in one direction, and half that amount in the opposite direction. The "Net Force" would be 500 pounds per second squared in the direction of the larger Force. A Force (push or pull) on an object

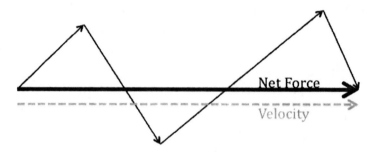

changes the Momentum in the direction of that Force. The sum of the Forces (Net Force) determines the final direction of the Velocity.

Velocity contributes to positive Momentum as it is Velocity in a consistent direction. Every time there is a course correction, Momentum toward that fixed point is diminished. So, Net Velocity is the overall rate of movement towards the objective, not just the speed

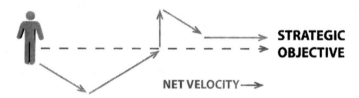

in any direction. Ultimately, Relationship Momentum is the Equity times the Strategic Velocity. Therefore, when Velocity is misdirected, strategic Momentum suffers.

The application for Relationship Momentum toward a fixed goal is obvious. There are many Forces in your life and business, and not all are pushing you toward your objective. You may be pushing hard toward your goal, but there are Forces pushing in alternate directions as well. Frequent course corrections also kill momentum toward your strategic goal.

Let's return to the formula for Relationship Momentum, $Rm = E^3V$ as an expression of Momentum. It's not just any Velocity. Running in circles won't get you anywhere, no matter how fast you run. Net Velocity, with respect to a fixed objective, is a measure of Momentum toward that objective. It is not just Velocity in any direction, but Velocity in a particular direction. I call this purpose-oriented Velocity, or "Strategic Velocity" (V_s).

Incorporating the concepts of Net Force and Net Velocity, my formula is stated as such: Relationship Momentum is the product of the Three Equities (Brand, Value, and Ambassador) times your Strategic Velocity. Stated as a formula, it looks like this:

$$Rm = E^3 V_S$$

Momentum is a simple concept that can be used to measure the progress and potential impact of any idea or endeavor. Whether you are a book salesperson or the CEO of a Fortune 100 company, your ability to identify, create, and manage the elements of your business relationships that contribute to (or detract from) Momentum toward your objective is by far the best predictor of future success.

6
VISTA COLOSSUS

"You can often measure a person by the size of his dream."
— Robert H. Schuller

Perhaps the easiest concept in these pages to understand is the relationship between Mass and speed to Momentum. What is more imposing, a loaded dump truck speeding down a hill or a wheelbarrow? Think of it in terms of impact. What is the hardest thing to stop? What will burst through almost any kind of road block? What is going to cause the biggest dent? The energy and degree of Motion of the dump truck is measured by its Mass and speed.

The energy and Motion behind your dreams can be measured in a similar way. How weighty are they, and how fast are they moving? I took a look back to 2012 at a series of events in the Middle East that have come to be known as "The Arab Spring." We saw the Mass (or the masses) of people, the speed with which ideas and ideals were spread, and the intensity of those ideas fueled by generations of oppression. Good or bad, the energy created an unstoppable movement. Compare that to a lone voice crying out in the wilderness. Size and speed really do matter.

Whether you are trying to kick start a revolution or launch a small project within a small company, the weightiness of your ideas and the force with which you can bring them to bear on your objective will determine the impact you have on the nation or on the company. In other words, the dent you make with your product, project, or purpose has everything to do with the movement of your dream and the substance (size) of your ideas.

Plenty of people have great ideas about how to change the world or how to advance their careers, but the ideas never go anywhere. They don't spread by word of mouth or by marketing campaigns. Sometimes it is because those ideas or proposals are not effectively communicated, or they may be too complex for people to understand. That is to say, there is no contagion and no speed of movement because the ideas are not packaged in a way that is easily transferable. Their idea is stationary and stagnant.

Empty dump trucks are large and have great capacity, but when they are parked and empty, there is no Momentum. In fact, no matter how weighty the idea they carry, without movement, there is no energy; there can be no dent. It's when they are loaded and moving that they carry tremendous Momentum.

In the context of our study, Mass (size) is illustrated through relational magnitude. Imagine a large truck with three containers, which represent three elements of your idea that give it weight and substance. These three accumulations are what I call the Three Equities, which are the strength of your Brand, the perceived Value of your product, project, or purpose, along with the effectiveness of your Ambassadors.

Let's be honest. Some ideas don't gain any Momentum because of their substance. They are simply just unworkable or ineffective. They don't get traction with people and don't gain any Momentum because they are not based on felt needs.

YOUR DREAMS: SIZE, SUBSTANCE, AND MOVEMENT

It takes a lot of effort to build a big dream. It also takes a lot to hold fast to it against every kind of obstacle. The biggest mental and emotional test is then pushing that dream forward into reality. As you get older, people tend to refocus their vision. An executive in his fifties is looking at a smaller window of opportunity than someone in their mid-twenties. But just because the range of vision is refocused doesn't mean the intensity has to change. Some people even get more determined as they grow older, even though their range is shorter. Why shouldn't they? They actually have more empirical evidence of how and why products, projects, and visions attain success.

I have a close friend who has been very instrumental in the writing of this book. He epitomizes an entrepreneur who has the means (recently sold his business) and the cerebral accomplishments to simply coast through his next 25-30 years. He could hang it up and enjoy the rest of his life without the headaches and the day-to-day shrapnel that ideation and new business ventures provide. My friend took a few months to travel and pontificate on his next venture. He decided to thrust himself into an even bigger project than his last — a product that could reshape the landscape of the health bar industry. Why do that at 50+? It is what he does. He is fulfilled through many things, but one of them is creating and then executing the next impossibility. God gave him a passion that he desires to master and fulfill.

THE PREFRONTAL CORTEX

The part of our brain known as the prefrontal cortex controls the executive functions — decision-making, futuristic thought, vision-casting, working toward a defined goal, and the orchestration of actions in accordance with internal goals. In other words, it is the part of our brain that does the heavy lifting when it comes to producing a purpose, pursuing goals, and turning a vision for the future into a present reality.

Like most muscles in the human body, if you do not exercise that specific part of the anatomy, it will atrophy. In this case, if you don't exercise your "vision muscles," you will lose the ability to dream big, as well as the ability to push those dreams into reality.

People also lose the ability to dream big because they have allowed it to be conditioned out of them. How can an elephant in captivity be tied to a small stake in the ground when it has the power and size to crush a small car? The animal's will and ability to think bigger than its surroundings has all but disappeared. Why do many prisoners who have been behind bars for years fear getting out? Why do many people from lower income neighborhoods fail to ever enlarge their territory and capacity? The prefrontal cortex is in atrophy. The challenge here is to have the audacity to think bigger than you see yourself and to realize that you can do almost anything if you are willing to dream big, derive strategy, and then add Mass to your Brand, your Value Proposition, and your Embassy of Ambassadors.

7

THE SPEED OF MIGHT

"The great weight of the ship may indeed prevent her from acquiring her greatest velocity; but when she has attained it, she will advance by her own intrinsic Motion, without gaining any new degree of Velocity, or lessoning what she has acquired."
— William Falconer

I had a football coach who gave me some great advice. I asked if he thought I could become a professional football player. He didn't try to be delicate, and he didn't beat around the bush. He simply replied, "You can't coach size and speed." I took that as a definitive "no," as it was evident that I was not going to become much taller or faster. The physics of football are a lot like the principles of business

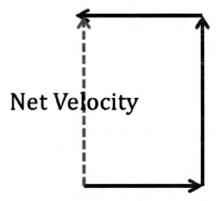

Net Velocity

success. If you get to the level where they play for real money, being bigger, faster, and stronger are basic necessities. The difference in the two is that genetics plays a lesser role in business. Success is a result of being in the right place at the right time and applying speed instead of having it as a physical attribute. You don't win by going fast in the wrong direction and winding up in the wrong place. I would argue that in business, "You can coach size and speed!"

Velocity is the speed at which you are traveling in a specific direction (at a given moment of time). The average Velocity relates to your average speed and direction over longer periods of time. For instance, when driving home for Christmas, you might travel 20mph east over a period of time, then 70mph north, then 30mph west. Your average Velocity would be something around 40mph north.

Net Velocity is movement of an object in a particular direction within a given time frame. For instance, a runner sets off on a jog, periodically changing directions as he runs. At the end of one hour, he has traveled one mile from where he began. The Net Velocity would be only one mile per hour. Strategic Velocity and strategic Momentum do not come from simply moving fast, but moving fast in a consistent and purposeful direction.

Think of a company that has consistently outperformed analysts' expectations and its peers in the marketplace. They have accumulated such strong Brand reputation, market presence, and following, that it would take years to decelerate their progress, even if all the factors contributing to positive Momentum were reversed.

Managing Momentum in a business is a lot like piloting an ultra large crude oil tanker. Today's modern ships measure over 1,000 feet long and weigh more than 500,000 deadweight metric tons. It takes a very long time for these mammoths to get up to speed, but once they get going, they will plow through the roughest seas without spilling the captain's cup of tea. The turning radius is so wide that it requires more than a mile for a supertanker to make a 180-degree turn. While turning is difficult, it is almost impossible to stop one of these ships. The Momentum is so great that most supertankers turn off their engines about fifteen miles from the dock. Imagine having that kind of power behind your idea or your company.

What large companies gain by the Momentum of their enormity, they lose in flexibility and nimbleness. You cannot steer a supertanker like a jet ski. It simply will not respond. A captain can spin the wheel in either direction, with no noticeable change in course. The only immediate result you will see from attempts at rapid course corrections is that the vessel begins to lose speed and Momentum. The point is that the larger your company or project, the more necessary a consistent strategic plan is to efficiently get where you are going. Your ability to correct your course without killing your Momentum has a lot to do with your ability to anticipate changes ahead.

The size and scale of your endeavor is also relative to your field or industry. A company with $5 million in annual revenues is relatively small compared to an NYSE-listed conglomerate. The smaller company can still be like steering a supertanker due to the fact that the company is the largest player in the local market and is understaffed to boot. I make this point to illustrate that the number of employees, volunteers, proceeds, or annual revenues is not necessarily always indicative of the size (Mass) of the particular project. The key elements have to do with the amount of time and energy it will take to maneuver.

Executives often allow themselves to be deceived by the power of their own Momentum. The fact that your tanker's Velocity is twenty knots doesn't mean that what you are currently doing is contributing to its forward Momentum. It only means that you were doing so about fifteen miles back. The very best product, project, or purpose leaders are constantly doing a couple of things:

> 1) They identify and constantly monitor the elements of their endeavor that contribute to positive or negative Momentum. They never assume that the engines are running efficiently simply because they are moving forward. They might be simply coasting on their own previous Momentum.

2) They constantly think about where they are going and anticipate course corrections fifteen miles ahead. The best leaders of large corporations or institutions commonly ask the one-hundred year questions. They think long-term because they understand what it takes to manage the forward Momentum of the organizations.

Here is the physical reality of managing the speed and size of business. Momentum is the product of two factors, Velocity and Mass (P=M x V). In order to increase Momentum, you have to increase either the speed or the size of your endeavor.

Like my coach advised me, slow and small will not succeed. If you are a small start up, you have to be fast and nimble to create positive Momentum. If you are a behemoth, you have to be vigilant about managing the elements that contribute to or detract from your forward Momentum.

I have worked with and for many CEOs and have seen three different types. One is like the captain of a supertanker who tries to steer it like a speed boat. Another is on a Jet Ski, steering as if he was aboard a cruise liner. With no sense of urgency, he does not take advantage of opportunities that present themselves. The third is the one who is comfortable in his or her own skin (the size of their ship), understands the amount of time it takes to build Momentum, and strategically applies Force to turn. Velocity is essential to building Relationship Momentum for your product, project, or purpose. What most people fail to recognize is that speed must be gained strategically and the size of the proverbial ship should be used as an asset rather than a liability.

8

THE GREAT HEADWIND

"Resistance is the most toxic force on the planet. It is the root of more unhappiness than poverty, disease, and erectile dysfunction. To yield to resistance deforms our spirit. It stunts us and makes us less than we are and were born to be. If you believe in God (and I do) you must declare resistance to be evil, for it prevents us from achieving the life God intended when He endowed each of us with our own unique genius."
— Steven Pressfield *(The War of Art)*

I travel back and forth to Africa from time to time, and I always marvel that it takes only nine hours flying-time to get there, but eleven hours to get back. It's not magic; it is Momentum. On the way to Africa we are often aided by a 150 mile-per-hour jet stream at our backs, but we fight it every mile of the journey home. A consistent headwind can impede or even completely diminish your Momentum. Relative to the earth, you are traveling slower but expending much more time and energy. On the other hand, a strong tailwind can push you along with such a force that it feels as if you are riding a wave. Things happen fast and without great effort.

Our goal is to create the optimum form of movement — Velocity in a consistent, strategic direction with the least amount of Drag we can incur. We want high efficiency in a straight shot toward our strategic objective.

Every business, every venture, every charitable initiative periodically needs to do an efficiency assessment to identify the headwinds and tailwinds. Take out a sheet of paper and on the left side list all the aspects of your business that you are able to accomplish with relative ease.

Now on the right list the hard stuff — things that seem to take forever, that suck the energy from you, or that never seem to get done right.

Don't be fooled by the obvious. If you think the easiest things to do are always the most easily done, you might be surprised. Usually, this is not the case. Hard and easy are comparative measurements relative to your strengths. Some of the more difficult tasks are for one group the easiest to pull off. For others, the simplest things turn into time-consuming endeavors that never seem to get done right — if they ever get done at all.

This is not necessarily a measure of speed. Remember that Momentum = Mass times Velocity. It is not just how quickly tasks are accomplished, but the product of speed and weight (significance). Let's say you operate a company that manufactures shoes. You have a great product, but the athletic shoe market changes rapidly. Fortunately, you have tremendous "Potential Energy" that resides in your ability to adapt to changing markets. Unfortunately, you also have a great weakness. It is only with tremendous difficulty that you manage to get out a product catalog, and it is rarely accurate. That creates all kinds of confusion and lost sales. As a result, Ambassador and Brand Equity suffer. So you see, the hard part, the heavy lifting (or the engineering) is done with relative ease. The challenge is a thirty-page catalog. Remember, hard and easy are comparative measurements. It is all about combined strengths and weaknesses.

There are many factors that can contribute to the relative ease in which things get done — intellectual capital, systems in place, business relationships, the corporate culture, etc. Generally speaking, the Three Equities are what contribute to positive Momentum — Brand Equity, Value Equity, and Ambassador Equity. Conversely, factors such as random course corrections, undercapitalization, lack of strategic capabilities or the absence of any of the positive Momentum generators will result in the greater impact of Drag in your endeavor.

There is nothing new about this list of factors. However, this little exercise can be a real eye-opener because it forces you to assess your business or your career in terms of physical movement, to identify the things that contribute to Drag as well as the sources of untapped Potential Energy. Potential Energy is the amount that you are able to change Momentum.

And do not be fooled by the insignificant. The office birthday party is completely insignificant compared to a new product launch. Or is it? To some that event might constitute the glue that holds everything else together. Most leaders are unaware of the Equities that contribute to Momentum in a company. You need to assess the headwinds and/or the tailwind at work in every aspect of your endeavor. When it comes to Momentum, everything matters.

THREE FORMS OF HEADWIND
The three forms of headwind are:
1) Habitual Headwind (Including but not limited to)
   a. Negativity
   b. Procrastination
   c. Complacency
   d. Jealousy
   e. Laziness
   f. Manipulation

2) Environmental Headwind (Including but not limited to)
   a. Internal Resistance
      i. Fear
      ii. Stagnation
      iii. Isolation
      iv. Scarcity Mentality

b. External Resistance
    i. Economic
    ii. Seasonality
    iii. Competition
    iv. Pricing
    v. Value

3) Resourceful Headwind (Including but not limited to)
    a. Staffing
    b. Funding
    c. Cash Flow
    d. Strategy
    e. Leadership

In the case of internal resistance, sometimes WE are the greatest source of Drag. This can be one of the hardest things to deal with because there is a kind of institutional endowment, which is another way of saying that owners feel entitled to fail in any way they choose. How many times have you heard someone say, "It's my company, and I will run it how I want?"

When you realize that hard and easy are comparative measurements that often reflect the strengths and weaknesses residing in your accumulated intellectual Equity, you may have to take a hard look at personnel. Do you have the team that can take you where you want to go?

You can look at every cycle of ideation like an international flight. The resisting headwinds that can appear in every project can derail your intended trip and even cause you to run out of fuel on the way to your destination. Drag is a given; it will always be on the peripheral looking to creep in. You do not have to be afraid of it, but you do have to deal with it. Once you make the commitment to face the issues on a regular basis, you can shift your focus predominantly to the positive things you must do to create your optimum Momentum.

9
IN THE CROSS HAIRS

"Clarity is the counterbalance of profound thoughts."
— Luc de Clapiers

My good friend, Mark, is the only survivor of the 9/11 World Trade Center attacks to join the Marines. Mark lost friends and colleagues on that dreadful day in September. He was fortunate enough to get out alive, but was fighting mad and anxious to serve his country in the war against terror. Within a week, Mark signed up to fulfill what he felt had become his destiny. After completing basic training, Mark shipped out to Iraq, ready if necessary to give his life for his country and his fellow soldiers.

Operating in a combat zone is very dangerous, no matter where you are deployed or what your assignment. However, Mark soon realized that the fighting in his sector had subsided, and his only job was to guard and patrol the highways between Baghdad and Fallujah.

Serving in Iraq turned out to be a lot of "hurry up and wait" and Mark was not being used in a way that was fulfilling his desire to fight or utilizing his training to engage the enemy.

Mark was in the best shape of his life. He was highly skilled with an M-16 assault rifle, several types of explosives, and sophisticated communications gear. As a U.S. Marine, he was trained to kill or subdue enemy combatants in a dozen different ways, even with his bare hands. He was determined, disciplined, and ready for battle. Though Mark served his country honorably, he returned home somewhat disappointed. Still enraged over the 9/11 attacks and the tyranny of the terrorist-friendly countries of the Middle East, Mark never got the enemy in his sights and never even fired his weapon in combat.

I can't relate to what it would be like to willingly volunteer for a mission that could include a hailstorm of bullets, adverse living conditions, and the possibility of death. But I can share the sense of the disappointment that comes from the lack of opportunity to perform, of what it feels like to be skilled, trained, and ready but never really able to engage in the pursuit of your highest objective. It's like being in a firefight and never able to return fire because you can't see the enemy. Or in Mark's case, being able to hear the gunfire but never being able to reach the battle.

Many people have invested heavily in the best training they could get. They also have a pretty keen sense of their personal strengths and weaknesses. Yet, for whatever the reason, they find themselves laboring away without being able to employ those core competences. That can be very frustrating, especially if your career path requires you to tack onto a heading rather than straight toward your strategic objective. Tacking back and forth, trying to make progress against a strong headwind requires a lot of patience and perseverance. At the same time, sailing a straight course to your strategic objective is exhilarating because of the quick progress you make.

Finding that place where you spend the majority of your time working at your highest skill level while being compensated financially for the Value you bring to the process — that is one of the greatest feelings you will ever have. Abraham Maslow called it self-actualization — being fully engaged using all your accumulated skills at their highest potential. For Maslow, that was the highest level of need and the most powerful source of personal fulfillment.

In terms of Motion and Momentum, you can think of this as a car with an eight-cylinder engine that's only firing on five. Push the gas pedal to the floor and you barely feel any increase in Velocity. Then suddenly, all eight cylinders kick in, and the surge of forward thrust throws you back in your seat. That's what it is like when you are doing what you are called, gifted, and trained to do. It fills you with a sense of power, Momentum, and forward thrust.

Take note — this is not all about making money because accumulated wealth and possessions are not the only measure by which we keep score. The highest sense of self-actualization for you might be teaching elementary school, working with underprivileged children, or writing the next great American novel.

Most people never get around to what they really want to do for one of several reasons:

1. They are so devoted to the pursuit of money and possessions that self-actualization has become an either/or proposition. Their values and perceptions force them to choose between feeling fulfilled and getting rich.

2. They have become satisfied with their own status quo. They sense that there should be more to their lives and relationships. They would love to be that person or to pursue those objectives. However, it is relatively safe and comfortable where they are, and getting to where they feel they should be is a risky and difficult journey. *This is good enough,* they say to themselves.

3. Some focus on the objectives they are pursuing with great passion and will never be satisfied until it is accomplished. They dream about it and talk about it all the time. However, that's all they do — talk and dream. You've probably met some talker/dreamers before. The absence of an action plan that has any chance of gaining traction turns their dream into a form of virtual reality. In other words, they have dreamed and fantasized about success for so long that they think they are successful.

You cannot have Momentum without traction. In other chapters I describe the commitment level needed to reach success. Momentum is more than that. You also need to be able to correctly identify and engage the target or relationship that will provide said Momentum. The opportunity must be in the cross hairs!

You might wonder whether you fit into one of these three scenarios. If you are reading this book and your endeavoring to inject some reality into your product, project, or purpose, the answer is — probably not. You're not looking for pretend success. You're looking for the real thing. So, let's get busy. You have been reading about the art and science of Relationship Momentum, and I want to make sure you are able take advantage of opportunities and make these concepts work for you. I do not want you to be frustrated and left unfulfilled like my friend Mark was. You are putting in the work and the training; I want you to be able to use it.

Below are your first four steps out of the starting blocks.

STEP ONE: There are three spheres of Relationship Momentum. You need to get these three areas aligned before engaging the formula in an initiative. In other words, they all have to point in the same direction in order for you to become efficient and effective in your endeavors. The spheres are:

> **The Spiritual.** Whomever you call God, (I recommend finding that out as I am sure He is worthy of the recognition), and whatever moral fiber has constructed your being, is the crux of being capable of acquiring Momentum. We are inherently relational; it's in our DNA to need communion with others. Your relationship with the Great Engineer is dire to your forward movement, as He provides a confidence and a communion that no art or science can explain.

The Personal. The Ancient Greek Philosopher Plato said, "Know thyself." William Shakespeare proclaimed, "To thine own self be true." If you are not taking time for yourself and to develop your gifts, the rest of this material is moot. If you do not love yourself, you simply cannot love others. If you cannot love others, you cannot create Momentum in your relationships and your endeavors will most certainly suffer. The personal sphere covers the realm of your closest relationships (friends, marriage, partners, with yourself, etc.) and is pivotal to building Momentum for your career and endeavors. This very important sphere has a large effect on your relational capacity and cerebral well being.

The Vocational. As illustrated above in Mark's story, vocational awareness is knowing yourself in terms of what you are uniquely gifted to do, and then being able to utilize those talents. It is essential to embrace our personal gifts in order to achieve actualization. Introverts often try to be extraverts, artists try to become engineers, and lawyers want to be novelists. You will never find that sense of self-actualization or highest level of personal success and fulfillment as long as you are trying to be someone you are not.

The root word for Vocation is *vocare*, which is Latin for "a calling." In other words, it's not just a matter of what you like to do or what you enjoy doing. It's a matter of what you are *called or destined to do*. It is that thing in your life that makes you say, "I have to do this." You may not know exactly why, but you just know that you cannot simply dismiss the idea. If you lay it down, it jumps back into the briefcase. You're not pursuing the product, project, or purpose. It is pursuing you! Whether it's for profit, for charity, or just for fun, "the calling" must be defined, the picture of success must be painted and the Relationship Momentum equation applied.

STEP TWO: In order to plug in a variable to the equation ($Rm=E^3V_s$) you first must identify what it is that you would like to get moving (i.e., increase Momentum). That means first identifying the primary target(s). Is it a product, a project, or a purpose?

> **A product** is a specific item that needs Momentum for placement, sale, or usage. An example I like to use is one of the greatest products of all time, the Chuck Taylor All Star. This timeless product is perhaps more en vogue today than when they were introduced in the 1950s. The canvas shoes that burst onto the scene more than six decades ago are still found in every shopping mall across America and have become an icon in the footwear industry.
>
> A product could also be a mutual fund, a car, a service offering, or even a new ribs recipe being introduced at a local eating establishment. The idea here is that you have a specific item that needs Motion behind it.
>
> **A project** is a specific enterprise or collaborative effort that is designed to achieve a given outcome or result. A great example would be a company that wants to increase revenue through a new seminar series. Or perhaps an initiative to increase awareness of a new health bar targeting golfers. A project is more of a tactical target as it possesses a beginning and an end. Project Momentum is often symmetrical with product Momentum, as there are many projects that include a product offering.
>
> **A purpose** is a vision, an intention, or an objective that can span years or even a lifetime. A purpose is a dedicated commitment to alter the course of someone or something. The best example that comes to mind is the Civil Rights Movement of the 1960s. This purpose was a vision of a man who had a simple dream that is still growing into the hearts and minds of people today. A purpose, however, does not always have to shape global culture. It can be as small as a local mandate to clean up the streets of

an older neighborhood, to start a new company that changes the financial advisory business, to become the dominant market player in the automotive industry or to better the education standards of a specific school district. A Vision may include products or projects in its strategy, but is much larger than our other targets, as it encompasses the desired outcome in its origination.

Remember this—you can have a product, project, or purpose in the same strategy, but the equation must be applied separately to gain the desired Relationship Momentum for your conquest.

STEP THREE: We are working to create Relationship Momentum. It is people who buy, endorse, tell and move ideas. Is this an internal or external application? Are you focusing on relationships within your company/entity/project or are you focusing outside of the walls of your organization and into the community? It is very important to know who and what you are targeting. It has everything to do with the strategy of your approach.

STEP FOUR: Once you decide what your target is and who you are targeting, you must take a step back, pull back the lens for a moment, and derive your point of origin. Without understanding your strengths, weaknesses, and the current status of your relational capital, how can you possibly know where you are and what you are capable of doing? Taking inventory of your relationships and strategically defining who is currently adding to or taking away from your momentum is imperative for your journey.

STEP FIVE: As important as your inventory and your point of origin is the need to clearly determine where you are going. You must define what success looks like. You must derive a picture of the proverbial "promised land" for your initiative. I refer to this picture as your "True

North" later in the book and it must be prominent as it is important for several reasons. When the odds get stacked against you and things are not going your way, you must have this picture of your destination in order to understand persevere through necessary pain. The picture of success must also be transferrable to those who are on the journey with you. If you clearly know where you are going and those who are helping you along catch the vision, you can truly keep success in the cross hairs.

My desire is for you to be able to apply these concepts in an arena that you were made to play in. I want you to avoid the frustration of missing the opportunity. Once you have begun to get some clarity on these spheres, targets and steps, you are ready to begin applying our equation — $Rm=E^3V_S$. The second section of this book is dedicated to the application of what I call the Three Equities. These are the variables that contribute to the Relationship Momentum of your product, project, or purpose, and hold the keys to the breakthrough you have been looking for.

10
BURN THE SHIPS!

"If you see the President, tell him from me that whatever happens there will be no turning back."
— Ulysses S. Grant

The year was 1519 when Hernán Cortez set sail for the New World. His strategic objective was the conquest of Mexico. The Aztec people were a great nation with vast stores of gold and silver, an incalculable prize for King Charles I of Spain. Though I do not agree with what he had set out to do (not all strategic objectives are noble), I do marvel at how such a small army could defeat a vast empire that had endured for 600 years. The key ingredient for their success would go down in history as one of the greatest Momentum tactics ever applied.

The Spanish conquistador first recruited his team for the great adventure and embarked on a dangerous voyage. After sailing halfway around the world, Cortez landed his eleven ships on the beaches of the Mexican Yucatan and unloaded the 500 men and supplies. Cortez then gathered his men around him and delivered those fateful words that now echo in the annals of leadership history, "Burn the Ships!" Certainly, none of his recruits had anticipated this. They must have begun to wonder, *Have we signed on to following a lunatic?* Irrespective of Cortez's mental state — if he was crazy like a fox or just plain crazy — from that point onward, there could be no retreat. The only option was success.

Ideas die from lack of faith, especially if the founders are the chief unbelievers. Burning the ships is synonymous with getting uncommonly serious about your objective. Relational movement in a consistent direction is what creates Momentum. Cortez knew that they could not generate break-through Momentum if his men were keeping one eye on their escape plan.

As you approach a point of no return, team members who have invested in the conquest usually begin to ask, "Where is the fall-back position, where are the reserves, what are the contingency plans?" Put simply, they wonder, "What if this doesn't work?"

I am indeed aware of the importance of risk management issues. I am also aware that many people have been engaged in a reoccurring cycle. A vision is born, the vision gets hard, and the vision dies. Then they try something else.

Most of us will try several things before we commit ourselves to a lifelong focused pursuit. However, the problem is often that many have never sufficiently invested themselves in order to create the kind of Momentum needed to be successful. They have adopted a tolerance or threshold for opposition and difficulty that is too low. They say to themselves, *I will do this, if it is not harder than that.*

I have bad news for you: there is no creative idea, process, or system so ingenious that it will work by itself. I cofounded and help to lead an association of independent inventors, and am fully aware of how rapidly new innovations are emerging. However, the reason an originator of an idea rarely becomes rich is because they are unable to incorporate or monetize their ideas. Rarely does the idea alone have the Momentum to become successful. As the old saying goes:

"Nothing works; people do."

The surest way to kill your dream is to not be "sold out" to its successful completion. That has been the cause of innumerable failed projects, including my own. On the other hand, it is this abandoned pursuit of the success at all costs that makes your vision contagious. Like Cortez, when it comes to entrepreneurs and inventors, there is a fine line between being considered insane and being celebrated as a genius.

You may not think of yourself as inventor. However, everyone who has high goals for themselves is in the process of creating a preferred future. If you do not have authentic conviction behind your ideas and ideals, you simply will not be able to create (or much less) sustain Relationship Momentum. You must have a relentless resolve to see that preferred future become a reality.

A great illustration of this principle comes from the Old Testament, chapter thirteen of the book of Numbers. Moses sent twelve men to spy out the Promised Land. Ten of those spies returned from their forty-day recon mission with what Moses called "an evil report." Their analysis was that the inhabitants of the land were like giants and that the men of Israel seemed like grasshoppers in their sight. Only Joshua and Caleb brought back a "good report," saying, "God is able to give us the land."

You've all heard this story. Here's the leadership analysis. Moses sent twelve men to spy out the Promised Land to see how they could conquer it. The essential difference between the ten spies and the two was their sense of mission. The ten went to see *IF* they could take the land; the two went to see *HOW.*

In an honest analysis, do you think that your level of commitment to your strategic objective will generate enough Momentum to overcome the difficulties, the obstacles, and the opposition in order to make it successful? If not, you have to ask yourself, *How much do I really want it?*

It is not *if,* but *how.* That was the attitude of Hernán Cortez. In burning the ships, he made sure everyone else had that attitude as well.

His reward was victory and riches beyond his wildest dreams. What are you looking for? Before embarking on the voyage, ask yourself this question, do you have any ships that need to be burned?

11
THE GREAT ESCAPE

"The important achievement for Apollo was demonstrating that humanity is not forever chained to this planet. Our visions go rather further than that."
— Neil Armstrong

To date, the Saturn V rocket is the only launch vehicle to transport human beings beyond lower Earth orbit. It remains the tallest, heaviest, and most powerful rocket ever brought to operational status and still holds the record for the heaviest launch vehicle payload.

Imagine yourself on top of a 6.5 million pound Saturn V filled with highly explosive liquid hydrogen. It's like being strapped to a bottle rocket the size of the Statue of Liberty. If a Saturn V were to explode on the pad, it would have the impact of a two-kiloton bomb.

You are about to be shot off of a launch pad, at which point you will accelerate from 0 to 272 miles per hour in the first 60 seconds. By the fourth mile, you've broken the sound barrier, on the way to a top speed of over 26,000 miles per hour.

At some point in the countdown, questions begin to come to mind: *What have I gotten myself into? Should I really be doing this?* But it's too late for that. You're already far too invested in the mission. You're buckled into the seat, they've bolted the hatch, and all systems are a go. Like it or not, you are committed to the process, and there is no way out.

As the Saturn V powers up to full throttle, you are already accelerating at such a rate that the g-forces cause your body weight to triple. The capsule will shake so violently that you have to clench your teeth because it feels like they will vibrate out of your head. Right when you reach the point at which you feel all hell is breaking loose, the capsule reaches a speed of about 17,000 miles per hour, or as astronauts call it, "parked-orbit Velocity." The violent shaking subsides and at that moment, everything suddenly becomes silent. The ride becomes as smooth as silk. The first great barrier is breached. Few people have ever reached this zenith. Even fewer have accomplished the bold feat that comes next. The final step is the "great escape". After several orbits, the engines reignite, increasing speed to about 27,000 miles per hour (gravitational Escape Velocity), and you literally crack the sky and head for the moon.

Escaping the gravitational pull of the Earth is a monumental undertaking. First you have to construct a spacecraft that can withstand the stress of that kind of friction and vibration. To propel a vessel of that size to that Velocity requires a rocket that produces almost eight million foot-pounds of thrust at liftoff. Anything traveling through earth's atmosphere at that speed and with that much propulsion behind it is in for a rough ride.

LAUNCHING YOUR INITTIATIVE

Launching a product, project, or purpose and propelling it to metaphorical Escape Velocity requires a lot of energy and effort, especially on the front end. Like the Saturn V rocket that propelled the Apollo spacecrafts, ninety-five percent of the fuel is spent in the first mile of the journey. Even while your project is still on the drawing board, there is lot of planning and testing that goes into a launch attempt. The human and financial risks are far too great to simply experiment with different methods until one of them works.

When you get it right, the initiative, whether a product, project or purpose, hits Escape Velocity and something wonderful happens. All the Forces that you have spent so much energy fighting to overcome — gravity, friction, and inertia (tendency of object at rest to remain at rest, Newton's First Law of Motion) — suddenly have little relevance. You are operating in a new environment with a different set of physical realities. And the view is magnificent!

THE FOUR STAGES OF THE MISSION
The four stages of launching a vessel into space correspond to the stages in launching a product, company, or a vision in such a way that it will attain Escape Velocity.

Stage One: The Launch
How you launch your initiative is the most important stage. Every mission has to allow for some mid-course corrections. But you have to generally be on the right trajectory. There can be no radical turns. Some will tell you that having all the answers doesn't matter — just do something and figure out the details later. That might work if you're painting a fence or engaging in any other endeavor that does not require a great deal of capital investment. In a major launch, however, margins are very thin. According to John Glenn, after traveling over 240,000 miles, Apollo 11 settled on the lunar surface with about five seconds of thruster fuel remaining. They had one shot, and the corrections required to find a suitable landing spot left them five seconds from disaster. Very few product launches are so capitalized that owners/entrepreneurs can make major course corrections without running out of fuel. Aim carefully.

Stage Two: The Big Burn

It is hard to anticipate every eventuality. Having poured over your calculations and completed your due diligence, you're ready. Hopefully you have not forgotten a critical component. You know the amount of fuel, food, and oxygen required for the launch. Needless to say, it is much easier to obtain those essentials before you launch rather than after you are under way. That is analogous to various kinds of intellectual and relationship Equities you need to have onboard before you get started. Once you're fully supplied and launched in the right direction, it is time to go to full force to where the majority of your fuel is spent. That simply means investing a tremendous amount of energy and effort. This is where planning pays off, because this stage requires hard work, long hours, high investment, and little profit-taking.

Some launches never reach Escape Velocity because the originators simply get tired of working so hard or get anxious to start taking profits. Or they get tired of operating so lean and begin spending before they can afford it. They consume the resources that would be needed for that second burn to propel them to Escape Velocity.

Stage Three: Orbital Velocity

Orbital Velocity is the stage at which you experience that weightless, quiet, and smooth ride. What a feeling! Your project is off the ground, and you no longer have to pour everything you have into propelling beyond the grasp of gravity. Now you can actually begin to turn a profit. But this is also where many launches fail to become what they could be. The owners of the idea miscalculated before the launch. They didn't realize how much fuel it would require, and they launched under-capitalized. Consequently, they ran out of gas before the second burn. Eventually, they begin to slow down and fall back to earth.

In the context of Relationship Momentum, many people fail in this stage as they forget the people (clients, Ambassadors, financiers) who helped them get to cruising altitude in the first place. It is also normal to see the Value Proposition begin to decline; this is why so many politicians lose their bid for reelection. If the Value Proposition suffers, the Brand is diminished and the Ambassadors lose their fervor. Escape Velocity is Relationship Momentum in its purest form and the final burn is what separates the legendary from the forgotten.

Stage Four: The Great Escape
Reaching orbital Velocity, the crew members are able to settle into a parked orbit. But the true magnificence of the journey is venturing beyond the earth's gravity. That, of course, requires another substantial capital investment (human and/ or monetary) to take them to the next level. Regardless of their original goal, many owners will reach parked-orbit Velocity, become complacent, and settle for an abbreviated objective. The companies, non-profits and products of legend (IBM, Microsoft, United Way, Salvation Army, The Hula Hoop, TiVo) are the ones that made the escape.

It is important to realize that the items that are being discussed in this book are equally important. All four stages are critical as you conduct serial launches within a larger initiative. This is why I describe our targets as products, projects, and purposes. Some visions (a purpose) have a multitude of product offerings and myriad projects (both internal/ external).

THE UNDER ARMOUR STORY

Under Armour, Inc. is a company that has not only established itself in the sportswear industry but has successfully passed through the four stages of a successful launch to Escape Velocity. They began with a small idea, took it global, and wound up dominating the market.

The mission of Under Armour's founder, Kevin Plank, was simple: to enable athletes to perform better. Plank started his empire by making shirts for football players that were much lighter and less absorbent than other undershirts. Their Brand Equity was built on this competitive advantage that Under Armour delivered to world-class athletes.

Plank and his company succeeded in the launch phase by carefully targeting a place in the market — sports apparel that actually increased performance. They got their products into the locker rooms and onto the backs of world-class athletes who became their Ambassadors. They achieved parked-orbit Velocity and started showing some impressive profits. But Plank was not satisfied with simply being profitable. By pouring in more advertising and endorsement dollars, they went from being profitable to dominating the market. Instead of just becoming a multi-million dollar company, they reached Escape Velocity and became a $1.4 billion behemoth.

There is a secret to why some ideas succeed and some fail. I believe we have found the answer. I want to provide you with the formula to leverage relationships and achieve greatness for your product, project, or purpose. I am going to show you how our equation and a concentration on the Three Equities can help your endeavors. I want to help your initiative, no matter how large or small, reach its maximum growth potential and escape from the proverbial pull of mediocrity. Hang on; it's going to be an interesting ride!

PART 2
E^3
The Three Equities

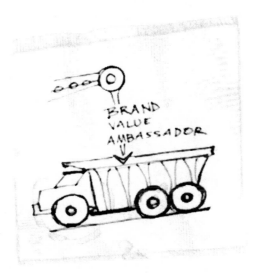

1

THE MATTER OF EQUITY

"We know the true worth of a thing when we have lost it."
— French Proverb

Have you ever noticed how success comes easily to certain people and for others, who work just as hard, success always seems to elude them? Momentum is a wonderful thing as long as the Momentum is carrying you in the direction you want to go. If not, it may feel like you are swimming upstream. Stop to rest for a moment, and you immediately begin falling back. Most people are trying to move forward against the resistance of a downward current. Progress comes only with enormous effort. For others, even as they continue to work hard, success seems to continually evade them.

So how would you evaluate the Momentum in your life and business? Is it naturally moving you toward your goal, are the waters stagnant, or are you swimming upstream? Your ability to identify, create, and manage the elements that contribute to overall Momentum is one of the most important factors determining where you wind up and how hard you will have to work to get there.

Formulas are simply shortcuts to understand the dynamic relationship between two or more things like Mass, Volume, Acceleration, Velocity, Gravity, etc. As previously stated, the concept of physical Momentum is determined by an object's Mass and Velocity. But how closely can these laws of the physical world be associated with intangible concepts like relationships, success, and strategic objectives? Obviously, they are not the same thing. I use Newton's Laws of Motion as metaphors for personal and professional growth. However, I have taken it a step further. Instead of simply using physical Momentum as a single-point illustration of career advancement, I am suggesting that the variables used to understand and predict physical Momentum correspond to identifiable variables in the business world.

Newton's formula states that physical Momentum (P) is the product of Mass (M) and Velocity (V) or P=MV. My formula states that Relationship Momentum (Rm) is the product of total Equity (E^3) and Strategic Velocity (V_s). The two formulas look the same, but note that I have replaced Mass in Newton's formula with the concept of Equity. So how is it that I came to understand the business concept of Equity to be synonymous with the physical concept of Mass?

EQUITY AS MASS

Equity can be defined as the amount of ownership in an endeavor. It is also referred to as the ownership in any asset after all debts associated with the asset are paid off. That is not unlike Newton's "Net Force." If you have Forces acting on an object in three different directions, the Net Force is the sum of all those factors. In terms of financial investments, the total Value minus the debt equals the Equity or "net ownership."

I like to think of Equity as the net worth of an asset that has accumulated over time. Using this financial term to describe less tangible business concepts is nothing new. Terms like "relationship capital" and "intellectual capital" are common in today's business talk. Intellectual capital usually refers to the knowledge and experience that has been accumulated in a company's employees or patents. You could also call this your intellectual Equity or property.

"Brand Equity" is the general feeling developed over time that the public associates with your company's name and/or logo. Business leaders know that the strength and weight of these intangible Equities usually have more to do with a company's long-term success than money, buildings, or inventory. Richard Branson once said, "I've never been particularly good at numbers, but I think I've done a reasonable job with feelings. And I'm convinced that it is feelings — and feelings alone – that account for the success of the Virgin Brand in all its myriad forms."

With regard to the substitution of Equity for Mass in my formula, the first assumption is that these intangible Equities have real weight, which is a factor in creating Momentum.

The Mass of an object is a measurement of its total matter, irrespective of its Volume. This means a little ball can have just as much or more Mass than a big ball, depending on the density of the matter. I love the play on words "Mass" and "matter." When it comes to Momentum — Mass, not size, is what really matters. Lots of people talk big about their dreams, their visions, and their plans for success as if those ideas possessed such great Momentum that they could sweep them into success with little effort. But the truth turns out to be that there is little weight (or Equity) to their ideas — just big talk without a lot of substance. That is like a big ball that has little Mass. They have a large vision, but when it comes to intangible Equities such as Brand Equity, relationship Equity, or Value Equity, they are lightweights. Think of vision as Volume and Equity as Mass.

MEASURING INTANGIBLE EQUITIES

If the strength of your Momentum is the accumulated strength of intangible Equities such a Brand Equity, intellectual Equity, etc., then a key to success is to understand how to identify, create, and manage those factors. There are many elements that can directly affect the size or scale of the Equity present in a project, product, or purpose. Here are four:

1. You have to understand where the Equity came from and be able to produce a blueprint of where to find more. The funny thing about older companies trying to recapture past Momentum is that executives rarely understand what created the magic back in the glory days.

An older manager might say, "I remember when we used to visit all our customers every month, selling was done face to face, and deals were sealed with nothing more than a handshake."

"That's it!" says the new CEO, and off they go visiting customers, shaking hands... and going *bankrupt.* There may have been a correlation between those activities, but visiting and shaking hands did not create the magic or the Momentum.

In order to sustain business or personal Momentum, you have to be able to accurately identify what Forces contribute to positive Momentum and what Forces create the Drag. That is not as hard as it seems *IF* you begin to evaluate relationships and business functions in terms of contributing to or detracting from positive Momentum.

2. You have to direct accumulated Equity of those intangible(s) in order to sustain Momentum. Let's go back to the concept of Strategic Velocity (Vs). It's not just any Velocity that contributes to Momentum; it is Net Velocity toward the fixed objective. If you speed off in a direction that veers away from your objective, it usually reduces overall Momentum.

CEOs often try to increase profits by leveraging their hard-earned Brand Equity to establish another product line. Sometime it works, but all too often one of two negative things happen:

a) Some of the Brand Equity invested in another product line is lost and consequently, so is Momentum.

b) Other times the Brand Equity is maintained, but the new venture represents a movement (or Velocity) in a direction that diverges from the objective. After a few years, managers realize that the company has wandered from its core competency and its core vision. As a result, that product line is sold or discontinued. Remember, Momentum is Equity *multiplied* by Strategic Velocity. The Brand Equity did not suffer badly, but because of the divergent course (Strategic Velocity not directed toward the objective) overall Momentum was diminished.

3. The power of compounding Equity of any kind is not only the eighth wonder of the world but is also the secret to future growth.

Earlier we identified three key Equities: Brand Equity, Value Equity, and Ambassador Equity. In real life, Relationship Momentum is affected by the product of these and other Equities. In my formula, E^3 is the product of these Three Equities or Brand Equity x Value Equity x Ambassador Equity.

That means that if any of the variables are zero, the product of the three will be zero. That also means that a manager's ability to make all three of these elements work together synergistically increases Momentum toward the objective. Synergy has come to mean that the sum of the parts is greater than the whole. That is another way of saying that Equities working together have a multiplied impact, not just an additive impact.

4. You have to manage your Equities in such a way that they are profitable. Initially, that sounds like simple budgeting and cost-control. However, it is a little more subtle than that. Reducing expenses does not necessarily contribute to long-term profits. In the same process by which you identify factors that contribute to Momentum toward the objective or contribute to Drag, you have to evaluate whether expenses are a sound investment that create Momentum or are simply a Drag on profits. It's not just a matter of cutting cost; it is gaining an understanding of strategic investing.

HOT AIR BALLOONS

A great many success books and seminars promote a secret to success based on big dreams, expensive clothes, and aggressive promotion. In short, if you want to be a success, just act like you already are. If you do this consistently, that is what you will become. There are a lot of variations of this supposed formula for success, but it boils down to: *"Think as if you are successful. Make others think you are successful. Then you will become successful".*

The way we think about ourselves and our businesses does indeed contribute to our success. However, success formulas based on appearance rather than substance are formulas for building hot air balloons. They produce public personas with large Volume but little Mass — big vision and profile, but without substantial Equity. General George Patton once said, "Walk softly and carry an armored tank division." The Mass of your combined Equities equals the weight in your Relationship Momentum formula.

2

BRAND EQUITY

"It's not slickness, polish, uniqueness, or cleverness that
makes a Brand a Brand. It is truth."
— Harry Beckwith

Brand is the first of the three essential Equities that contribute to Relationship Momentum. The word "essential" indicates that any one of those Equities is ineffective without the other two. A great Brand and a defective product is a lost cause. So is a high-Valued product without an effective Ambassador. By restating the formula: RM = (Brand Equity x Value Equity x Equity Ambassador) x Vs, we note that Relationship Momentum equals the combined product of Brand, Value, and Ambassador Equities times Strategic Velocity.

Brand Equity is the emotional side of Relationship Momentum. It is often unpredictable because, like love, it is a fickle thing. Why people love one product or cause is not clearly understood. Relationship Momentum occurs when someone or something closes the affinity-affection gap. At some point (and sometimes for the oddest and most unpredictable reasons) people cross an imaginary line and enter into the loyalty zone. It's just like entering into a relationship with a person, except the relationship can be with a product, project, or purpose. Some of these relationships are more committed, more trusting, and more monogamous than others. Whether we are flirting, dating, engaged, or married to the product or the cause, it is indeed a relationship.

Someone who has been dating the same person for a long time might ask themselves, "Where is this relationship going?" This is another way of saying, *"What is the Momentum, the Drag, and the Potential Energy of this relationship?"* We all (hopefully) know that deep, trusting, long-term relationships are not built on looks alone. People fall in love with someone or something because of an Ethos, the essence of what it is or who he/she is. Perhaps you should look at your product, project, or purpose and consider its "inner beauty." What goes on behind the façade? Or as some say, "If you saw how the sausage was made, would you want a taste?" Are people as likely to fall in love with your Ethos — the how and why you do what you do — as they are with your image? That is precisely what Volvo drivers, Mac users, Boston Whaler boaters, and Starbucks drinkers have done. To one degree of another, they have entered into a relationship with the Ethos of product.

Some companies even incorporate their Ethos into the actual name of the company or product they provide. Take FUBU for instance. The clothing giant founded in 1992 by Daymond John is a perfect example of demonstrative Brand Equity. The name of the company, FUBU, stands for: For Us By US. The company was founded on the premise of offering a better product for less. The product was made predominantly for those who loved the culture and the lifestyle of Hip Hop by those that loved the culture and lifestyle of Hip Hop. The Brand was adopted by powerful marketplace Ambassadors and soared to unbelievable heights. In 1998 the company reported more than 350 Million in sales, and has amassed more than 6 Billion in global sales to date.

The same Brand Power is true for causes like World Vision, the Olympic Games, and Habitat for Humanity. It is also true for grand projects such as an election campaign, the Apollo space program, or the Bill and Melinda Gates' Foundation's crusade to eliminate malaria. It is a relationship with the organizational Ethos, and the dynamic of those relationships has created sustainable forward Momentum.

LOGOISM AND PAVLOV'S DOGS

The first belief about Branding that needs to be pulled down is what I call "logoism."

True and false propositions:

Your Brand equals your logo.	— FALSE
Your logo is a statement of who you are.	— FALSE
Your Brand Ethos is who you truly are.	— TRUE

As I have already said, your Brand is your Ethos, the fullest statement of who you are. People don't fall in love with logos, but they do create committed relationships with Brands and are fiercely, defiantly, and sometimes irrationally loyal. The signature look and color of a logo definitely have a powerful effect, but much like the effect on Pavlov's dogs. Ivan Pavlov (1836-1946) was a Russian psychologist and the father of classical conditioning. Pavlov demonstrated his ability to condition a response (dogs salivating) by pairing it with a stimulus. First, he paired the introduction of food with a repeatedly ringing bell for a period of time. Then he rang the bell without the food, and the dogs salivated. But if he stopped introducing food for a period, the conditioned response would begin to be "extinguished." Classical conditioning, also known as stimulus-response or operant conditioning, is the fundamental principle underlying advertizing and logoism — pairing the logo and the product. The most effective marketing campaigns go a step farther by pairing the product with the Ethos of the company. The result is that people enter into a committed relationship, not with the car, the coffee, or the computer, but with the

Ethos of the company. Those corporate or personal Ethos connections are more long-lasting and harder to extinguish.

Of course, the science behind much of advertizing today has been lost along the way. There is often no effective attempt to condition the stimulus (the bell) to the actual reward (dog food). Instead, we fixate on creating bigger, louder, and prettier bells. People do not fall in love with logos and images without actual rewards or experiences to which the stimulus can be tied. In other words, you can spend a truckload of money, but you can never teach dogs to salivate with only the sound of a bell. The only way they are going to love that bell, or your logo, is if they associate it with a positive experience. And what experience could be so wonderful so as to make them salivate whenever they saw or heard something that reminded them of your product, project, or purpose (i.e., your logo)? It is the weight of your combined Brand and Value Equities.

BECOMING AN ICONIC BRAND

Early on, I suggested that among your existing relationships, there is enough potential Relationship Momentum to propel you to the next level. The idea is to cultivate the true relationships you have rather than the imaginary ones you think you need. The same idea goes for a Brand and an emblem. In most cases, your logo is good enough. You are not trying to come up with an iconic Brand, because a Brand is more than an image; it is your Ethos. So the objective is to make your Brand Ethos iconic by the habits, the standards, and the organizational culture — even if the organization is just you.

My father and I have enjoyed a long-term partnership with Converse and their lighthouse product the Chuck Taylor All Star. The star on the side of the shoe is not the reason the product has become an icon. The shoe has stood for those who have questioned the norm for decades. The All Star Brand is more about uniqueness than it is about looks, comfort, and even price. In 1947 the Converse shoe company did not create an iconic Brand. They created an Ethos around a product that became a Brand.

PERSONAL BRANDING

American Historian Daniel Boorstin once said, "An image is not simply a trademark, a design, a slogan, or an easily remembered picture. It is a studiously crafted personality profile of an individual, institution, corporation, product or service." A Brand could also be thought of as a story that is being developed and enhanced over time. Companies and organizations have their Ethos-Brands and so do individuals working within them. It's kind of like a sub-Brand or supporting Ethos, a supporting role in the cast or a subplot to the story. One of the easiest ways to tell if you are in the wrong job (i.e. the wrong story) is if the personal Ethos-Brand you are trying to develop does not complement the corporate Ethos-Brand — the story the company is trying to tell.

I have spent seventeen years in the financial services business, but I have never been known as "a financial guy." That's not my story, my Ethos, my Brand. I am known as a business Ambassador who creates Momentum for others via relational capital. The result has been that people come to me with issues that can only be solved through relationships and Momentum. When my personal Brand of Ethos complemented the story the company was trying to tell, I was very successful. When the story and Ethos changed to something incongruent with my own, I knew immediately it was time to move on.

Personal Ethos Branding is something that comes from inside, not a tactical response to your environment. You have to know yourself and be comfortable with who you are. There are people I know who are working very hard to establish themselves in an industry or a particular company. But personal Ethos and personal Branding seem to be a secondary rather than a primary driver. They are playing off of every other personal Brand-Ethos around them except their own. As a manager, it was hard for me to tell if those employees were in the right job, the right company, or even the right industry. They first needed to figure out who they were and what personal Brand of Ethos they were trying to develop, i.e., what story they were trying to tell.

NON-STOP BRANDING

As Warren Buffet so eloquently put it, "Your premium Brand had better be delivering something special, or it's not going to get the business." Errol Flynn said, "It isn't what they say about you; it's what they whisper."

Perception truly is reality — at least for a while. What they whisper about you today, they will shout tomorrow. Many people mistakenly assume that Branding is something that only takes place during the initial launch of a product, project, or purpose. However, Branding is like a river. It's a never-ending flow that must be sustained and enhanced while being managed, maintained, and protected. In building Relationship Momentum, one must concentrate their substance and Ethos more so than pomp and circumstance. Your Brand is the foundation of what you are bringing to light. Your Brand-Ethos is the tip of the spear of your personal or corporate initiative. It must be built and handled with extreme care.

3
THE ART OF WHY

"Art is the imposing of a pattern on experience, and our
aesthetic enjoyment is recognition of the pattern."
— Alfred North Whitehead

People want to buy products that work, follow leaders who produce results, hire employees and contractors who perform, and support causes that make a real difference. Simple as that, right?

Well, actually no — it's not that simple. There is little evidence to suggest that people operate as purely rational agents. As a business executive who has recruited and managed hundreds of professionals, I can tell you that the best candidates don't always get hired and the best employees don't always get promoted. As the cofounder and Chairman of the Aslan Guild, an intellectual property and product development group, I can tell you from experience that many of the best products never make it to the market. As the former Board Chairman of a non-profit organization, I can assure you that the most efficient and effective organizations do not always get the most funding. Why people do what they do, and why things work the way they do is a combination of emotion and rationality (of art and science).

Great people, and quality products that also embody an Ethos of purpose, can hold a powerful attraction. This is more than just wearing a tailored business suit or launching a slick marketing campaign. *Why* they do what they do is completely integrated into *what* they do. Not only is it integrated into the way they do things, the *why* that drives them is as evident as *what* they do.

People are drawn to that kind of integration of *what* and *why*. They do not merely want to use a quality product or hire the productive person; they want to be associated with a person, product, or company that combines a *why* that is highly purpose-driven with a *what* that is highly effective. It is the seamless flow of the "intangible why" and the "concrete what" that gives a person or product the Momentum toward strategic objectives.

IMAGE ABOVE INGENUITY

Take Apple, Inc. for example. The Apple commercial introducing the Macintosh that premiered during the 1984 Super Bowl is one of the most famous of the last several decades. Hundreds of people marched in like robots and sat transfixed before a huge screen on which an ominous dictator appeared. It was an image reminiscent of a scene from George Orwell's *1984*. One defiant individual being chased by the thought police charges the screen, throws a sledge hammer, and destroys the power that held everyone captive. Then the Apple logo appeared.

The Apple Brand represents disruptive technology to a culture discontent with the status quo, one that is fully willing to discard the norm in order to find the best solution, one that challenges the notion that we should do things just because they have been done that way for years.

People were initially attracted to Apple as much for their corporate culture as for the quality of their software and hardware. "Think Different," was the marketing campaign slogan behind a product launch a few years ago. It's true that when one tries the Apple products, they are often hooked on the innovative technology. But even when there was almost no business software being written for the Apple operating systems, some people began buying Macintosh computers for their businesses. They bought into the Apple culture despite functional limitations. Even today, Apple fanatics will admit that some aspects or applications may not work as well as they do with other products. Nonetheless, they would never consider abandoning their commitment to Apple. That level of Brand loyalty among customers is very rare. This is Relationship Momentum in its purest form. The product of Brand Equity and Value Equity resulted in Apple's tremendous Relationship Momentum with customers. It was created by the seamless combination of culture and craftsmanship — science and art; what and why; product and purpose.

RELATIONSHIP MOMENTUM WITH EMPLOYEES

The same principle that creates Relationship Momentum between a company and its customers has a similar impact on a company and its employees. Below is an all-too-familiar illustration of how that works:

Let's imagine an employee named Bill. Energetic Bill is a great worker who is really fired up, not only about his own success, but also about the success of the company. He thinks about innovative solutions at home, talks shop to his wife as long as she will listen, and brainstorms in the shower. All this makes Bill one of the company's best producers. Over time, however, the employee-company relationship begins to deteriorate.

One of Bill's problems was that he got carried away working on his ideas. Though he was at the coffee shop working on company projects long before the office opened, he was often late for work. The conflicts grew between Bill and his manager who began focusing on Bill's consistent procedural violations. There were several conversations in which Bill responded to the manager's procedural request with the question, "Why do we have to do it that way?" The manager's immediate response: "Because I said so."

Pretty soon Bill's attitude toward work drastically changed. Instead of being purpose-oriented, he became task-oriented — that is, what Bill cared about was simply doing what he was required to do. Following the rules precisely became his personal mission. The company's success became his secondary concern. Projects were not as exciting, the clock ticked much slower, and at 5:00 p.m., Bill was the first one out the door.

So who was to blame for the deterioration in the relationship between Bill and his Company? In actuality, Bill and his manager both shared in the responsibility. Without the seamless flow between the what and the why – *between the procedure and the purpose* – Relationship Momentum between Bill and the company greatly diminished. Bill continued to fulfill the job requirements, but the energy and the Momentum was gone.

A counter example is the reemergence of the American automobile industry. Back in 1970 and 1980, American-made cars were considered significantly inferior to Japanese and European Brands. One of the problems was the manufacturing process. Workers were considered extensions of machines, doing repetitive tasks all day. There was no incentive to approach their jobs as purpose-oriented employees. They were like task-oriented Bill.

American manufacturers began organizing workers into teams that participated in decisions about how to assemble cars most efficiently with the least defects. In other words, they connected *procedure with purpose*. The result has been that American made cars have equaled and, in some cases are beginning to exceed, their previously superior competitors.

Brand Equity (Ethos) as well as Momentum for a product, project, or purpose is generated when the procedure and the purpose flow seamlessly together. The same is true for an individual and his/her career objectives. People spend countless hours, and sometimes a lot of money, trying to figure out what they want to do. By comparison, they have barely thought about why. The standard answer has to do with making money. However, you will rarely find a person or company that has gained Momentum from their personal or corporate Branding when that Branding was solely about making money. There is a higher purpose for them — and for you.

4
THE ELEVATOR

"It is only at the first encounter, that a face makes its full impression on us."
— Arthur Schopenhauer

I was on an elevator once with Cal Turner, Jr, the former Chairman of Dollar General. He had no idea who I was, but I certainly was aware of the person with whom I was riding. Overhearing my conversation, Mr. Turner turned to me and said, "So what exactly is it that you do for a living?"

I froze.

I had recently launched my first consulting practice. I knew what I was trying to do with the service I provided, but it would have taken me half an hour to clearly explain it to Mr. Turner. Instead, I hemmed, hawed, and bumbled through a synopsis of how I worked with business owners — blah, blah, blah. He listened politely, said "Good day," and got off the elevator.

Talk about a blown opportunity. More importantly, I missed the chance to make an impression, to plant the seed of a relationship that I could begin to cultivate. Instead, I looked and sounded like a novice (which I was) in front of one of the country's most respected retail giants. Ironically, great business leaders are often interested in everything anyone is doing. They soak up information and business intelligence like a sponge. That's why Mr. Turner asked me what I did for a living. Who knows, perhaps the CEO of Dollar General had asked ten people that day what they did, looking for someone who would inspire him. To that individual he would have replied, "Tell me more." I received no such invitation, and it was painfully clear that nothing I said had gotten any traction.

I vowed never to be in that dreadful situation again. Before the next person asked me that question, I was determined to have a better answer. I needed to be able to quickly paint a picture of what I did that was clear, but intriguing enough to make them want to say, "Tell me more."

To do that I followed the advice of a mentor of mine, John Nickodemus, who taught me the 3 B's of presenting.

Be Brief —Don't try to give them your entire business plan, don't look desperate, and most importantly, do not exhaust your time! If you have a one-minute opportunity, take thirty seconds and shut it down. If your audience gets the feeling you are going to talk their ear off, they will never ask a follow-up question. At that point, they're just trying to get away from you, and they will make it a point to avoid you in the future. That is definitely not the preferred outcome.

Keep in mind that it is the detail that you don't reveal that intrigues people and makes them want to ask follow-up questions. And that is the goal; to be sufficiently intriguing that it begs for a follow-up question, as well as sufficiently brief that they have time to ask for more. You don't want them to feel so threatened by your verbal barrage that they dare not ask for more information. If after your elevator speech people do not ask a follow-up question, you have either failed to be brilliant or failed to be brief. With Mr. Turner, I failed at both. Being asked for more information provides you with the license to answer as well as the license to ask a reciprocal question. This becomes the foundation on which to build a productive business relationship.

Be Brilliant — Have a clear presentation that holds an element of mystery and intrigue. Most rookie elevator speeches are characterized by over-the-top excitement, thinking that this enthusiasm will attract followers. However, the better approach is one of competence and clarity. Unlike my answer to Mr. Turner, your answer should demonstrate that you are an authority on the subject. The answer should be targeted at a genuinely felt need, and provide a solution that could be easily understood. Good elevator speeches tend to focus on the highest purposes. For instance, when a real estate agent is asked what he/she does, the answer might be something like this: "I enable people to arrive at good decisions about the most important asset and purchase in their lives."

The response from someone on your elevator might be: "What is the most important asset or purchase?"

Instead of jumping to a presentation about real estate, the salesman might answer: "It's their home. My system is built on using my experience to educate my clients as I advise them through the process of buying or selling."

The most effective elevator speech then leads to a follow-up question that is the entre into a full conversation. Remember, Relationship Momentum is not created by talking *AT* someone, but by getting some to talk *WITH* you.

Be Gone — Knowing when to stop and when to disengage is an essential part of darn near everything, including first impressions. Each of us needs to cultivate a sense of Relationship Momentum. The best time to disengage from a conversation and wait for a response is when the Relationship Momentum is at its peak. Do not over talk your welcome. Don't kill the moment with your mouth.

In Branding yourself, a product, or an initiative in general, you only have one opportunity to lay the original path in which you or it will be received. One shot. That's it. This is actually the internal aspect of the Relationship Momentum dynamic. One form of Relationship Momentum is the degree to which your relationships propel you toward your strategic objective. In that sense, relationships are a means to an end. The other form is more internal — the Momentum of the relationship itself. You cannot effectively build and manage the former without the latter. The art comes before the science. In other words, the science of Momentum from relationships is dependent on the art of building meaningful relationships.

My father always used to say, "Before a purchase, there is always pain. Whether the purchase being made is cerebral or tangible, your elevator speech needs to be able to touch someone in their place of pain." Your product, project, or purpose is a lake of fresh water for a burning fire in someone's life. If it's not, it is forgettable. When someone asks me today what I do, I tell them, I am a Business Ambassador. I help people create Momentum via relationships and human capital.

As I write this book I am currently working with a phenomenal company that happens to be the fastest growing financial firm in the United States. My specific duty is to help them grow organically within their current offices. However, my elevator speech with a new prospect or company is never, "Hi, my name is Brian. I work for ABC firm and I am looking to recruit new talent to our office in Boca Raton, Florida." It's brief, but it sure as heck is not brilliant. The idea is to get a question in response, which in turn, provides you with the license to answer but then return a question for a question. This is often the proverbial building block for a new and profitable relationship.

Elevator talks are needed for sales people, individuals, consultants and large corporate executives alike. They are imperative even for people launching a new initiative or project within their company. The Branding of an idea's validity is always tied to its first impression.

Brand Equity is enhanced by the elevator. It is the portal to building Ambassadors for your initiative. You cannot have Ambassadors until you can first clearly identify and communicate your Value Proposition that defines and supports your Brand Ethos. Second, you have to train others who can clearly regurgitate it at a moment's notice. Most communication gets lost in translation or improvisation. Your speech must be repeatable before it can ever go viral.

If your pithy platform presentation follows the three B's the receiver will ask for more, and that is when you get a chance to discuss your deliverable, as well as probe for more pain.

Whether you are communicating to one or many, selling or buying, or are introducing an idea or raising support on a project, you only have a brief moment in time to set the tone of how your initiative will be received. About the amount of time it takes to ride up a few floors on an elevator.

Be Brief, Be Brilliant, Be Gone!

5
VALUE EQUITY

"Try not to be a success, but rather to be of Value."
— Albert Einstein

Value Equity is the second of the three all important Equities within the Relationship Momentum Equation. It is Value that supports the Brand. It is Value Equity that is the glue and the foundation for your creation and accumulation of Ambassador Equity. Without Value, your product, project, or purpose will live a very short life.

There is a Danish fairy tale by Hans Christen Anderson that tells of an Emperor who cared for nothing more than his wonderful clothes. One day, a pair of swindlers came to town and boasted of a special cloth that was invisible to those who lacked wisdom. Concerned over whether or not he could see the clothes himself, the Emperor instructed two of his servants to view the cloth. The servants were too worried to admit that they could not see the clothes, and they pronounced their brilliance.

The Emperor then clothed himself in the imaginary garments and proceeded to parade himself through the town. The townspeople, also hearing of the fallacy surrounding the cloth, did not want to appear unwise, and they too praised the Emperors garb. Finally, a child near the end of the precession shouted, "But he has nothing on." The people began to whisper until everyone watching the Emperor began to shout, "The Emperor has no clothes!"

The fairy tale was crafted to illustrate the truth that is often found behind the eyes of a child. Children often see through the pomp and circumstance, the proverbial noise of a situation, and can clearly expose its true identity. Despite the power of the Emperor and the Brand of the office he held, he ultimately became a laughing stock. Everyone realized that his greatness was no more than a façade. When true Value is present, it is not hard to see. It is pure, and it is real.

Changing of the Guard

I was recently told a story of an officer in the US Department of Commerce who worked with the Chinese. The officer was unique in that he took the time to not only become an authority on the products and services he represented, but to also become a student of the customs and protocol of his ecosystem. He was well respected and had an incredible personal Brand. His Value Proposition was strong and his Ambassador Equity with the Chinese was at an unprecedented level.

The officer eventually retired from his post and was replaced by another very capable officer of commerce. The new officer, while skilled at his work, did not conduct his affairs with the same level of excellence and respect as his predecessor. He thought that he was only there for commerce, but seemed to forget that the key to his success was in building and maintaining relationships. His attention to the customs and sensitivities of his surroundings waned and the Value Equity suffered. The result was a strained relationship with the Chinese and a decreased number of American imports in the region.

This is a great lesson for any CEO, business owner, territory manager, or person in a position where past and current relationships must be stewarded. The Brand can be the greatest in the world, but if the Value Proposition of the past is not honored in the future, Motion is often lost.

Price and Value

Many people mistake cheapness with Value. Just because something is inexpensive or at least less expensive than its competitor, does not mean that it translates into Value or Value Equity. We have all heard that price is an issue in the absence of Value. This is true. If your only Value is your margin of price or cost, you will not be able to adequately support your Brand or acquire internal or external help. We are looking to create Relationship Momentum. Price and cost are important, but they do not make people want to shout your story from their platform. Remember this: Value is much more than a fair return or equivalent in goods, services, or money for something exchanged.

People form relationships and loyalties to the products they consume. They often become emotionally attached to the ideas and ideals they support. Value is the element that holds and draws the relationship nigh.

The Bonding Agent

Let's return to my good friend and client who is developing a never before seen, sports-related, health bar. He initially ran into problems keeping his ingredients in bar form. He had an uphill battle and searched for a solution for over two years. His goal was to have a 100% certified organic bar that was gluten free. Gluten is a proven bonding agent on one hand, but is quite unhealthy for digestion on another. You can see his dilemma. No one wants to buy a health bar that crumbles. Eventually, he found an organic, healthy and tasty bonding agent. It has become his trade secret and I can attest to the quality of the product.

Value Equity is the bonding agent for your ideas and your initiatives. If the Value can be created and communicated, you then have the power to exploit your Brand and acquire Ambassadors for it. Value Equity is tough to attain, and as my friend experienced, you may not always be able to use the same ingredients as the rest of the crowd. But, the fact that your product, project, or purpose is different is what often makes it, well…valuable.

6
TRANSCENDENTAL VALUE

"The reinvention of daily life means marching off the edge of our maps."
— Bob Black

Anyone can (as they say) "bring Value to the table." Value is not hard to establish. Simply create a needed service or a product and lower the price until you establish Value. Of course, we are looking for more than just Value. We are looking for Value Equity. We want to build and sustain a robust Value Proposition that thrives and expands over time.

The long-term goal is to establish relationships where trust and Value Equity are continually deepening based on the product or service you deliver. So let me rephrase the statement about the Value on the table. The ability to create and maintain Relationship Momentum over a long period of time is based on your ability to bring increasing levels of Value to the table. Or as we call it, Value Equity.

Let's be realistic. Some business initiatives are fundamentally flawed. In the current business environment they have little or no potential Value. In other words, you can't build a business making widgets when the cost of production is greater than what the market will bear. And you can't offer a commonly available service that is more costly to perform than what people are willing to pay. Of course, business environments are not static, but constantly changing. The United States sits on top of more oil trapped in shale than the sum total of all the oil fields in Saudi Arabia. But the price of oil, the political environment, and the current technology previously made extracting that oil a losing proposition. Only when the price of oil decreases and political will and technology advance can that business model have the potential to create Value. That is unless the product is vastly superior to the competition.

That's a familiar concept straight out of Introductory Econ class. However, there's more to creating and sustaining Relationship Momentum than supply and demand. It's all about sustaining long-term relationships by increasing Value Equity. The reason Relationship Momentum diminishes with customers, clients, and all kinds of personal relationships has more to do with attitude than innovation, more about complacency that competency.

Here is a typical business scenario illustrating how many business relationships come to an end: The owner of XYZ, Inc. makes a pitch and lands a service contract. Excited about the new client, XYZ begins doing their very best to deliver on the agreement. If you think my illustration is going to suggest that those at XYZ became complacent, lazy, or too busy with other clients, you would be wrong. Even after several years, XYZ continued to do an excellent job for their old client.

There's a psychology as well as a science to Relationship Momentum. Newton's First Law of Motion states that bodies at rest tend to remain at rest, while bodies in Motion tend to remain in Motion, unless they are acted upon by an external Force. The Second Law is related to Force and Acceleration, i.e. Force equals Mass times Acceleration. The Third Law states that for every action, there is an opposite and equal reaction.

Those three Laws of Motion together explain why in a rapidly accelerating automobile, the driver and passengers can feel themselves begin pressed back into their seats. Force is measured in terms of g-Force, the multiple of the Force of Gravity. Likewise, Newton's law explains why at a constant speed without Acceleration, the passengers of the automobile feel no sense of Motion. If they feel anything at all it is the vibration of the road. In a vacuum (in space orbiting the earth), they have no sense at all of movement or Momentum, even though they are traveling at 18,000 miles per hour.

The psychology of Relationship Momentum works in a similar way. When the XYZ was getting up to speed on their new business relationship, the client felt the effects of Acceleration. They had a very real sense of the Momentum of increasing Value. XYZ was effectively addressing a felt need. However, as XYZ continued on at same speed, the client felt no sense of Momentum. The sense of Value and Relationship Momentum began to wane. Some new executives at the client company decided it was time to entertain bids for the service XYZ had been providing to see if anyone could provide the service as a lower cost. In other words, they were looking for some added Value and knew nothing of the previous relationship with XYZ. The actual Value of XYZ's service had not diminished, but the sense of Value and Relationship Momentum had.

If your product, service, and price remain stagnant, there is no sense of positive Momentum. In fact, when the price increases, which it inevitably will, the sense of Value tends to diminish. A sense of Relationship Momentum is the result of continuing to add Value to the business relationship. Note that I am not talking about advertizing and promoting the Value you bring to the table. I mean actually increasing it. Banks and brokerage firms are often notorious for this It makes investors wonder: *If they spent the money creating more Value rather than advertizing it, my feelings and experience with that institution would be a lot better.* Every business cycle, every invoice, every renewal, I have to ask myself: *What can I do to increase the Value I bring to the table.* I know that if I don't do that, the relationship will grow stale... The sense of Relationship Momentum will diminish, and they will soon become former clients.

It is important to note that I am not talking about up-selling, but rather about upgrading the Value of your current agreements. I have found that creating an accretive Value Proposition has helped me to continue increasing my Value Equity and Relationship Momentum.

7

THUNDER AND LIGHTNING

"And when I breathed, my breath was lightning."
— Black Elk

The chief of an Indian tribe was closely observing a young warrior who was quickly coming of age. The young man was beginning to assert himself, trying to establish his own identity and place in the tribe. Not unlike many young men and women in the business world, the young warrior was bold and confident, determined to demonstrate his manhood and garner respect for his voice. However, in doing so, he would often interrupt others before listening to what they had to say. While his aim was to demonstrate his maturity, he actually conveyed the opposite. It was obvious to all that he enjoyed listening to himself more than anyone else. This element of self-awareness evaded him.

The chief pondered how he could instruct the young warrior to listen more and talk less. Simply pointing it out would not have helped. The young warrior did not have the ears to hear. So the chief took him out to an open field in the middle of a thunderstorm. Being much attuned to the Forces of nature, the two Indians knew well the inherent dangers. Every time a clap of thunder boomed, the young warrior would flinch in fear and look to the chief. The chief never flinched but only continued to calmly nod and smile as he watched the sky.

Finally, the young warrior asked the chief why the thunder did not frighten him. The old man said, "It's not the thunder that concerns me, it's the lightning." As soon as he had spoken those words, a lightning bolt struck the top of a nearby tree. The sound was deafening, the air tingled with electricity, and sparks flew in all directions as trees exploded and fell to the ground. The warrior looked again at the chief. He remained calm but was now staring into the young man's face.

The chief said to the bold young warrior, "Words can be like thunder — loud but useless. Or they can be like lightning, which comes suddenly with a flash of light and can bring down even the mightiest of trees."

PREGAME SPEECH

During a round of golf, Terry Crisp, Hall of Fame NHL Player/Coach, told me about some of his more memorable moments as a coach of the Calgary Flames. One of the most memorable pregame speeches of his career was delivered by his captain and future NHL Hall of Famer, Lanny McDonald. McDonald addressed the team seconds before the sixth and decisive game of the 1989 NHL Stanley Cup Finals. The Flames' captain stood before the team for several seconds as if overcome by the moment. He chose his words very carefully. McDonald simply said, "Win!"

If the Calgary Flames had lost, McDonald's words (or word) would have been quickly forgotten. But they won, and his short but impactful pregame speech has become legendary.

THE HARD TRUTH

One of my mentors, Jim Shoemaker, once told me, "You want to be a man of substance and not flash." Initially, I took offense at what Jim was implying. But the truth was that at that time in my career, I did have a habit of shooting off at the mouth, making extravagant claims of what I intended to do. Eventually, I learned the lesson of the young warrior. Don't fall in love with your own voice. Don't be so engaged with formulating your next comment that you do not hear what others are trying to say. Listen first. As it has been said, "If you are primarily engaged in listening rather than talking, you'll know everything you know and everything others know too."

Whether you are in a group or in an intimate setting with an individual, remember that the volume of words that come out of your mouth has absolutely nothing to do with the Value of what you know or what you have done. Mark Twain once commented, "Thunder is good, thunder is impressive; but it is lightning that does the work." In a world where most products, projects, and visions are more thunder than lighting, we should remember that true Value lies in what is done and not necessarily what is said.

8

THE DELIVERABLE

"Businesses that are wrapped up in themselves make for very small packages."
— Gary Church

How many over-Valued companies, employees, or products have you come across? In many of those cases, the insiders and stakeholders are a little detached from reality. They have convinced themselves that who they are or what they have to offer is of far greater Value than an independent evaluation would support. This is particularly true for private companies and even more so for startups and start outs. Needing to bolster self-confidence, they are more inclined to tell themselves how great they are.

Independent feedback is like a mirror; it reflects a true picture of who they are. People get so wrapped up in creating their own reality that they miss the fundamental elements that contribute to Value. Your product, project, or purpose has to form a relationship with the consumer, and subsequently, with sustainable Momentum.

I once consulted for a firm whose executives were so convinced of their company's superiority that they would virtually ignore marketplace competition. They were completely self-referencing; they only compared themselves to themselves. They actually produced a strong service, but it was not packaged properly for their Ambassadors to exploit. Their service was similar to others in the space and they were offering it at a premium cost. It was as if they expected people to line up around the corner to work with them. Relationship Momentum consists of the Three Equities that are multiplied by each other — Brand Equity, Value Equity and Ambassador Equity. The true Value of a product or service has to take into account the ability of your Ambassadors to share the story. In the ultra competitive landscape of the new economy, many times, you must be both better and cost sensitive. You have to begin thinking of the Relationship Momentum equation as a whole. To say that you will have a successful product without a robust deliverable or Value Proposition is a self-deception.

The company with which I was consulting ended up being nothing more than a bundle of solid intellectual properties run by a group of people who separated product Value from the realities of the marketplace. The result was that they continually patted themselves on the back for a great product and became expert commentators on why there was no Momentum. The basic reason was that their product lacked the Value Equity needed to support their Brand's claims and to acquire industry Ambassadors.

Four Laws of Value Equity

Whatever the Value Proposition, or the deliverable you are creating, there are four irrefutable laws of Value Equity that must be reassessed frequently and religiously.

1) It must be real. Contrary to popular belief, the consumer is smart. If your Value is not real and robust, they will know.

2) It must be relevant. No matter how well it works, there has to

be a significant felt need in marketplace. It is not enough for you to simply want them to have it or to totally believe that they need it.

3) It must be transferable. If the Value Proposition is not easily transferrable from person to person, it is not something an Ambassador can effectively represent.

4) It must escalate. If the Value Proposition does not grow, you will become vulnerable to competition and to losing clients and even Ambassadors.

The Real BP

A prime example of the Value not being real was demonstrated through the ineptitude of British Petroleum (BP) during the Deep Water Horizon oil spill of 2010. BP has claimed for years that it was the environmentally friendly oil giant and even went as far as to change their colors, profile, and marketing campaigns to reflect that Value Proposition. However, the world would soon find out that "the Emperor had no clothes." BP Chief Executive Officer Tony Hayward's less than apologetic remarks about the disaster demonstrated this. Not only was he unapologetic for equipment that was outdated and untested, he remarked in a live broadcast that he simply "wanted his life back." Hayward's statement exuded a sense of arrogance and exclusivity that stuck to BP just like the crude oil stuck to the beaches and plant life in the Gulf. It was as if Hayward was saying that he was annoyed by the interruption of millions of people whose businesses and livelihoods were destroyed. If true Value is not rooted in the Ethos of a company, eventually the Brand gets exposed.

Perhaps at one time, BP was the company it claimed to be. Perhaps, it was all Hayward's doing, though not likely. In any case, a great gulf had formed between BP's actual and perceived Value, and fixing it had not been a high priority.

The Blueprint

A good example of maximizing the three Laws of Value is the growth of one of the country's prominent church-planting organizations,

Every Nation Ministries. The movement was started when three men decided to use their complementing gifts to create a model built on discipleship and the duplication of Ambassadors for their mission: to spread the gospel to Every Nation in their Generation.

The Value Proposition they created gave their disciples a voice and a platform for those who had a vocational calling to serve in the pulpit, on campuses, and even on the professional playing fields. The Ambassador Equity, first created internally and then channeled externally, provided an unstoppable amount of Momentum and created an entire nation of Ambassadors for the mission.

The founders of Every Nation Ministries understood the need to develop a model that could grow by Osmosis, and be fueled from its growing number of Ambassadors. This acumen to grow exponentially was not the only recipe for success. According to their co founder, Bishop Rice Broocks, it was the commitment to building Spiritual Family that was the difference maker. This is similar to large successful family run businesses or models built on training the next generation. Companies like Hobby Lobby and Wal-Mart have built their organizations on a commitment to raising up the next generation and providing everyone in the family with a voice and the opportunity to fulfill their destiny.

Every Nation Ministries was first founded by three men in a living room in 1994. They now have 1,500 Churches in 60 Countries worldwide. Growth and Momentum on this level is possible when the Brand is strong, the Value Proposition satisfies the four Laws of being relevant and transferable, and the mission's Ambassadors are positioned to tell the story and to duplicate themselves. Every Nation exemplifies Relationship Momentum in its purest form and has demonstrated on a global scale how to make their ideas and mandate move!

The Reality of Value
There are three kinds of reality — yours, mine, and actual. Perception can substitute as reality for a time. However, it is for a very short time. Eventually, by experience and reputation, consumers are going

to discover your true identity. Many times startups have to inflate their image just to be recognized. What many entrepreneurs, as well as established businesses, fail to understand is that they have only a limited amount of time to bring up the measure of true Value to the level of perceived Value. The greater the Velocity of your product, project, or purpose, the faster true Value has to catch up with perceived Value. That same principle is true with all forms of Equity — Brand, Value, and Ambassador. If true Equity falls short of perceived Equity in any of these areas, making up the shortfall is the first order of business.

9

AMBASSADOR EQUITY

"An Ambassador is not simply an agent; he is also a spectacle."
— Walter Bagehot

In 1815 the Congress of Vienna officially recognized Ambassadors as having extensive powers to control the flow of information, maintain diplomatic relations, and project the influence of their chief executives. The word Ambassador comes from the Latin root word *ambassarre*, which means to send. King Ferdinand of Spain was the first to employ these accredited envoys. When one of his emissaries arrived on foreign soil, he was treated like royalty because he spoke directly on behalf of the king. His words and his influence were direct extensions of the one in power.

Just as we need Ambassadors for our national diplomacy, our initiatives need them to "speak on behalf of the king." Today's Ambassadors come in all dimensions. Many of them are consumers who like to share the experiences they have had with your product, project, or purpose. Some might be coworkers who have a vested interest in your success. They all share one thing in common: they are ordained to evangelize the world for your endeavors.

THE APPEARANCE OF AN AMBASSADOR

Ambassadors carry the flag of their sender. They wear the clothing, eat the food, and tell the stories of their senders. Did you ever think you would see a day when the emblem of a computer company would be more common than the bumper sticker for your favorite sports team? Times have changed. Modern day product Ambassadors will promote their favorite consumption as if they had founded the company themselves.

Ambassadors know implicitly the story of their sender. They know the elevator speech and the Value Proposition backwards and forwards, and can recite it at a moment's notice. This is incredibly important when the Ambassador is trying to persuade his/her host on the king's new idea.

Ambassadors adopt the Brand Ethos of the sender. This is really extraordinary when you think about it. Individual consumers adopt a product Brand as their own and identify themselves with it. Whether it's a computer operation system, a sports apparel company, or a rock band, passionate Ambassadors become personally identified with a Brand Ethos. "I'm a Nike guy," one might say.

Ambassadors are internal and external. Ambassador Equity is maximized when there are true emissaries who are nearest to the Brand and can affect the Value Proposition. The internal Ambassadors become fanatics as their faith in the Value Proposition overflows. The more proudly they feel about the deliverable, the more movement you will see on all fronts. Without these internal Ambassadors, the external Ambassadors will eventually question their own allegiance to the product, project or purpose.

Ambassadors use many forms of communication. A handshake and a face-to-face conversation will always be the best way to communicate. However, technology has given Ambassadors myriad social media tools to make known a Brand, Value Proposition, or a story to its target audience.

In a world where social networking is no longer the exception but the rule, the quality and quantity of the content you provide for your Ambassadors becomes fuel for the engine to create Momentum. Content is a context for conversation, conversations lead to relationships, and relationships lead to initiatives gaining Momentum.

The Unlikely Ambassador
You can mark the moment that an idea breaks free from the crowd by the appearance of the "Unlikely Ambassador." This is a person who would not normally associate with the product, project, or purpose, but who unexpectedly brings fanatical enthusiasm to the table. It is the sixty-year old millionaire businessman sporting a pair of canvas Chuck Taylor All Stars. It is the 300-pound ex-NFL player who buys a Snuggie and then tweets (Twitter) about it. It is the Hollywood actor and diehard democrat who says, "You know what, that republican is the better candidate for our country," or vice versa. When the Unlikely Ambassador appears, the crowd takes notice, the pendulum swings, and Relationship Momentum in its purest form is created.

Ambassadors are critical in the drive to create Escape Velocity, which is Relationship Momentum in its purest form. Escape Velocity is when no natural Drag can stop the Motion that has been created. Very few initiatives ever reach these phenomena, but when it happens, it is a magnificent spectacle.

During the Civil Rights Movement of the 1960s there was an unexpected group of Ambassadors who played an important role in the cause reaching Escape Velocity. The movement had one of the greatest Ambassadors of all time at the helm, Dr. Martin Luther King Jr. But even with Dr. King leading, a legion of Ambassadors was needed for the ideas and ideals of equality to become the rule instead of the exception. It was the actions of an unlikely group who helped the movement begin to escape toward success. The Unlikely Ambassadors in this endeavor were the American Jewish community who played a large role in the funding of the Civil Rights Movement. They were also instrumental in founding and funding some of the most influential civil rights organizations, including the NAACP. Rabbi Abraham Joshua was found arm-in-arm with Dr. King in 1965 at the March on Selma. The unlikely change agent was one that supplied the Unlikely Ambassador Equity required for the movement to survive and thrive.

Ambassador Equity is the epicenter of the Relationship Momentum concept. It is the energy within the nucleus of your concept and your ideas. If you want your ideas to move, you must acquire this Equity. You can have the greatest Brand delivering the greatest level of Value, but without someone to tell the story, you will never find the success you are after.

10
OSMOSIS GROWTH

"We are all susceptible to the pull of viral ideas. No matter how smart we get, there is always this deep irrational part that makes us potential hosts for replicating information."
— Neal Stephenson

Even though Google is one of the largest companies in the world, they have been known for small public-awareness budgets and a penchant for guerrilla marketing campaigns. Google's Gmail was first launched in 2004. Despite the size of its market today, the beginnings of the enormous email service were quite humble. They were, in fact, crudely inconspicuous. Admission to use the new Gmail service was only granted if you were invited by one of the current members who themselves were handpicked for the roll out. This type of marketing strategy, called "market scarcity," has been used for centuries to create interest and growth. However, this tactic has usually been employed in very elite and expensive social settings, such as affluent restaurants or private clubs.

This launch was not targeted to the affluent per se, it was for a free product that would ultimately be marketed to the Masses. The strategy worked, and Google redefined the word "viral" in terms of contrarian tactics. People simply wanted to know what was so great about the new product that you had to be selected by a current user to join. Gmail's Ambassadors created a global fire of interest. The product reached Escape Velocity, and Gmail is now the third largest email portal in the world.

Osmosis is a biological term that refers to the net movement of solvent molecules. In layman's terms, Osmosis is the physical process by which something moves net of the output of energy. Spreading the word by Osmosis (by someone else's energy) will always go farther, faster, and at less expense than organic growth (by your own energy).

Just as in biological Osmosis, there is the presence of kinetic energy (energy caused by Motion) within an idea that causes it to go viral. The key to Osmosis growth is that the creator of the idea is not the one expending the energy.

A close friend of mine owns a very successful recruiting firm. He is a big believer in the concept of developing Ambassador Equity and having business Ambassadors expand his territory. As he likes to put it, "I want to make money while I sleep." This scenario is where Momentum reaches its purest form. When the Brand is strong, the Ethos is true, and the Value is real.......Ambassadors will appear. And when properly equipped — the magic happens.

The referral or word-of-mouth concept is not new. It is simply a part of the reason why some ideas move and some don't. Everything we discuss culminates into this idea: Momentum feeds on itself. It's when a dependent top line revenue model becomes interdependent (not dependent on the creator). It is when a CEO of a financial advisory firm goes to Africa on Safari and returns three weeks later to find the pipeline larger than when she left it.

My father and I owned and recently sold an internet shoe company. One summer, upon returning from a vacation, a surprise awaited us.

My father checked his messages, and there was a voicemail from Bob Dylan, requesting a private shipment of sneakers. To this day we still don't know where the referral came from or where Bob heard about our niche service. It didn't matter. This was a perfect example of growth by Osmosis. An Ambassador somewhere told Mr. Dylan of our product, service, and capabilities. It was a great day for us. My father had put over thirty years into the retail industry and built a personal Brand on the ability to gain access to labels and styles that were rarely found in stores. He combined that with the Value Proposition of being able to get what you wanted within one week, anywhere in the world. This level of Brand, Value, and then Ambassador Equity allowed a company that started with a $10,000 investment and a few Chuck Taylor All Stars to be sold for close to one million dollars. Not a bad return on investment.

Google was successful with Gmail not only because they had Ambassadors. They were successful because they built an incredible Brand Ethos and had a very robust Value Proposition behind the product. This enabled them to build a legion of Ambassadors whom they had never met face-to-face. The Ambassador or emissary that operates on your behalf in person is very valuable. However, in an ever-growing virtual society, you must be able to build trust and loyalty through Value and Brand alone. When these Ambassadors are equipped with education and a winning strategy, a true marketplace marvel can be witnessed — growth by Osmosis!

11

THE BUSINESS AMBASSADOR

"An artist's sphere of influence is the world."
— Carl Maria Von Weber

Michelangelo devoted more than four years to the conception and completion of his masterpiece, *The Last Judgment*. It was indeed an extraordinary undertaking. The chief difficulty was not just the size of the famous piece of art, but the fact that it was painted on the ceiling of the Sistine Chapel. Michelangelo imagined and perfected the artistic technique of distorting images to create the desired viewer perspective. He also developed the chemical compounds to create the special colors needed for the project. He was able to accomplish his grand project only because he was centuries ahead of his time regarding both his artistic perspective and the science that it took to accomplish this timeless piece.

Over the years I have encountered a different kind of artist, whose masterpiece is not concocted on canvas but rather in the marketplace — One who creates commerce, movement, and Momentum wherever he or she goes; One who sees the hypothetical bands of communication before they exist and can make an unobtainable relationship feel like it's in the office down the hall. The artist of which I speak is the Business Ambassador.

The Business Ambassador may not always have an office, a benefits package, or a pension, but they carry the flag of the product, project, purpose, or people they represent. They are the Equity holders in a world where relationships make everything move. They are the economic relationships that can take ideas and ideals to places that the average salaried employee cannot. They are artists. Human capital is their paint, relationships are their brush and the marketplace is their canvas.

Their impact seems magical, because it combines a skilled use of both art and science.

However, it's not magic; it's Relationship Momentum. In the long run, it doesn't matter if they have experience or relationships in a particular field. Eventually, they turn relationships into human capital and human capital into positive movement.

Human Capital

There are many forms of capital that the Business Ambassador controls, but the most powerful of all is human capital. Human capital is the fuel that every company, every idea, and every deal runs on. Without it, there is no possible way to establish Momentum for a product, project or purpose. Just as there are brokers for other forms of capital, there are brokers, or as I like to call them, Ambassadors, for human capital.

The Business Ambassador sees every relationship as important. The Ambassador understands that the relationship must fulfill an economic, emotional, or technical purpose; however, if the relationship is of no immediate use, he or she knows that it certainly will be for someone else. Everything comes full circle in the Ambassador's world. The Business Ambassador's form of capital is extremely valuable as the Value can be recycled without a complex valuation placed on it. Utilizing the Business Ambassador and creating Ambassador Equity is not necessarily the easiest, but can be the quickest way to create Momentum.

Once your Brand and Value Equities have achieved some sort of scale, the next step is to acquire Ambassador Equity for your initiative. One way to acquire this Equity is through the acquisition of the Ambassador. You either have to buy one, rent one or recruit one. You must also become one yourself. It is very possible to transform into a real Equity player by doing one simple thing: Start becoming commerce instead of simply searching for it.

There is most definitely an art and a science to building Relationship Momentum. The art form deals almost exclusively with the role of the Business Ambassador and the acquisition of Ambassador Equity. They have been called diplomats, mavens, connectors, and centers of influence. I am introducing a new level of commerce emissary. I have chosen to call them Ambassadors as it is their job to be empowered to speak on behalf of the King. They are the arrows in your quiver. They create the movement for your product, project, or purpose and the first step to acquiring them is to learn the art yourself. You must begin to learn to be altruistically selfish by finding commerce for those whom you would eventually seek out for reciprocal efforts and opportunities. Translation: you must become one before you can make one. Remember this: it takes one to find one, it takes one to know one, and it takes an even stronger one to grow one.

12

THE AMBASSADOR HABITS

"Watch your thoughts for they become words. Watch your words for they become actions. Watch your actions for they become habits. Watch your habits, for they become your character. And watch your character, for it becomes your destiny."
— Prime Minister Margaret Thatcher

Successful Business Ambassadors can be identified and characterized by a series of habits, each designed to build and maintain Ambassador Equity and Relationship Momentum. Many Ambassadors do this without thinking. It is their art form. They concentrate on the objective of building Ambassador Equity and most everything else seems to fall comfortably into place.

FIVE HABITS OF AN EFFECTIVE BUSINESS AMBASSADOR
1. Business Ambassadors Make Every Recommendation a Personal Matter.

Business Ambassadors are not merely social media junkies with lots of friends and connections. They typically do not "like" or "recommend" casual acquaintances. While they often harness the power of social media and are skilled at using their influence in that forum, it does not accurately represent the Business Ambassador's genius and art form.

Pushing a button is a cheap and easy way of making connections that requires little or no investment or risk of one's own earned Equity. A personal introduction is, however, another matter. In such case the Business Ambassador is, in effect, putting up or "staking his reputation" on the Value that a person will consistently bring to the table. Business Ambassadors are in their element when they are making personal, face-to-face connections. This is how they connect the dots, advance the deal, make the introductions, and create Relationship Momentum. Consequently, one of the habits of successful Business Ambassadors is that they will either choose to make introductions eagerly and personally, or they will excuse themselves and do nothing at all. Effective Business Ambassadors are very protective of their Ambassador Equity and whether they use their influence through social media or in person, they will be very careful how and in whom they invest it.

For Would-Be Business Ambassadors: Every recommendation or introduction that proves its Value over the long-term increases your Ambassador Equity. Every frivolous or uninformed recommendation dilutes your influence. One bad recommendation can set you back years. Business Ambassadors are in the business of building as much Equity and influence as they can. They understand that Ambassador Equity is an essential ingredient in the formula for Relationship Momentum. Consequently, they take a careful and thoughtful approach to introductions and referrals and think of them as investments of their own. It is their capital.

2. Business Ambassadors Drive in Five Lanes of Traffic.

Several years ago I came up with the concept I refer to as "Five Lanes of Traffic." It is one of the habits I have gleaned from great Business Ambassadors. The purpose of the five lanes is for activity diversification and management. Imagine a race car weaving through traffic as it speeds around oval track at 210 miles per hour. The drivers are experts at drafting in order to save fuel, reduce stress on their engine, or sling shot around another car.

If you've ever been to a race at the Indianapolis Motor Speedway, you'll notice that after the race car pulls off the track, the orderly line quickly turns into a chaotic dash. The track at Indianapolis is five lanes wide, and the race cars use every one of them, searching for the optimum path.

Every entrepreneur, manager, or cause leader has to find his or her groove or lane in which to run. It's not the same for every person. Race cars are set up differently and so are people. The optimum path depends on the car, the business environment, the track, and the driver. Each one spends many laps in the early part of the race searching for it.

If you have ever been in the sales, distribution, or recruiting arena, you know that you need more than one lane of opportunity. You start driving all over the track until you find the unique groove — not necessarily a defined lane — but the most efficient path. The path that crosses back and forth over two or three lanes is the fastest way around the track. It is the one you have to find and follow if you are going to finish in the lead (win).

For Would-Be Business Ambassadors: There is a big difference between needing a Business Ambassador and actually becoming one. On one hand is an individual or entity that desperately needs help creating Momentum. On the other hand is the Business Ambassador who creates Ambassador Equity by helping others. For the Ambassador, the five-lanes-of-traffic concept has a different meaning. He is looking at five people, projects, or visions into which he can inject positive Momentum.

Remember this: the Ambassador is also not looking for one-way relationships. It's not even a two-way relationship they are after, but a mutually beneficial relationship that can help them compound their efforts involving numerous people.

3. Business Ambassadors Live by the Principle of Reciprocity.

The principle of reciprocity is a primary psychological motivator — so powerful that Dr. Robert B. Cialdini, author of the book, *Influence: Science and Practice*, indentified it as the most powerful of all weapons of influence. Put simply, giving a gift or volunteering some kind of service creates a powerful a sense of obligation to return (or reciprocate) the favor. Cialdini's book is full of examples from both controlled studies and real-life experiences of reciprocity being used as a compliance tactic to manipulate people into making the most bizarre decisions imaginable. Manipulation is not the goal for the Business Ambassador. It is, however, to apply the concept of being altruistically selfish. The late great Zig Ziegler once said, "If you help people get what they want and need, you can't help but to get what you want and need."

For Would-Be Business Ambassadors: Manipulating others for your own interests, whether by psychological influence or material defraud, is a onetime play. People who feel pressured may give in and comply, but they often resent it. Sometimes they get angry, most often angry with themselves for being manipulated. The response will be to avoid you like the plague. That is, of course, the very opposite of the Business Ambassador's goal which is to build long-term, mutually beneficial relationships. A genuine Business Ambassador employs the principle of reciprocity, but always benevolently. He's not a salesman, and he never obligates a business contact unless he is sure that person is going to come out as the beneficiary. Again, a good Business Ambassador understands that accumulating Ambassador Equity is one of the keys to increased Relationship Momentum.

4. Business Ambassadors Constantly Clarify Expectations.

This habit is an extension of the principle of reciprocity. An expert salesperson will align half a dozen cerebral tactics, subtly ratcheting up the pressure for you to say yes. Conversely, a good Business Ambassador has no hidden agenda. What need is there for a hidden agenda if your motivation is to succeed by helping others? The Business Ambassador must learn to become altruistically selfish. In other words, he has figured out that helping a select group of individuals, companies, or causes will in turn help him, his company, and his cause. Sometimes there is a quid pro quo (this for that). Sometimes there is not. But in every case, a good Business Ambassador makes it a point to state what is expected and what is not. In other words, it is more than merely telling the truth, it is being completely straightforward.

For Would-Be Business Ambassadors: Every aspect of a Business Ambassador's relationships and his ability to create positive Momentum on behalf others is built on impeccable integrity and trust. People need to be made aware of the limits and extent of your intentions. Most people view written contracts as a means of protecting a party's interests. However, a Business Ambassador sees things in terms of Relationship Momentum. Consequently, he views a written or cerebral (verbal) contract, not only as a means to secure his interests, but also as a means of protecting the relationship from misunderstanding. In other words, the relationship is more important than the deal.

The worst thing you can do in business is to defraud a partner, a client, or a friend. Talk about a Relationship Momentum killer! The second worst, and almost as bad, is to act with integrity but allow others to think they have been defrauded. The key word in that sentence is "allow." A Business Ambassador accepts the responsibility for clarifying and defining the parameters of any business relationship.

My literary coach, Walt Walker, shared a great example. As Editorial Director of a book publishing company, Walt also served as the chief acquisition editor. That means that he annually reviewed about 700 unsolicited manuscripts or proposals. A few days after mailing what they considered to be the great American novel, people would often call to find out if Walt had finished it yet. Since it seemed to him that the submission guidelines implied that a manuscript would be read, Walt tried unsuccessfully to persuade the publisher to adopt a NO UNSOLICITED MANUSCRIPTS policy. Every now and then a manuscript would make it past the initial screening of an assistant editor and land on Walt's desk. This prompted a letter or phone call from Walt.

Over the years, he learned that if he requested more information, more chapters, or some kind of editorial change, it would inevitably result in runaway presumptions. So he constantly found himself repeating the same conversation:

> "That doesn't mean the manuscript is approved."
> "It doesn't mean the book committee will like it even if the numbers do work."
> "We are simply looking for some more information."

Because he had learned about anxious authors' propensity to make optimistic assumptions about his intentions, Walt accepted the responsibility of going the extra mile to make sure there was no misunderstanding. Business Ambassadors understand that knowingly allowing people to harbor false expectations, even when it is in the Ambassador's interest to do so, is simply defrauding. Business Ambassadors are all about building up Equity and Relationship Momentum. That's why they are in the habit of clearly defining relationships and expectations.

5. Business Ambassadors Live by the Rule of 72.

When a Business Ambassador is engaged in a relationship or deal cycle (sales, recruiting, funding, etc.), he knows that he must maintain significant contact every seventy-two hours or the opportunity gets cold. Think of it in terms of professional football — as an offensive lineman blocking his opponent. Coaches continually impress upon their players to maintain contact and sustain their blocks. It not enough to simply fire off the line and strike a powerful blow. The play is only successful if the linemen can sustain their blocks.

As soon as you hang up the phone and begin celebrating an agreement, Momentum begins to wane. Many business deals collapse somewhere between the initial agreement and the finalization of the deal. Usually it is because the businessperson did not maintain contact or (so to speak) "sustain their block."

The same concept holds true for a fresh relationship. We have talked about the importance of a first impression. Almost as important is the attention paid to the development of the relationship in the early stages.

For Would-Be Business Ambassadors: If you are not a person who will consistently add Value to a client or customer, then you are unlikely to get beyond the casual interests of a Business Ambassador. If, however, a Business Ambassador does get involved with your initiative, it will be in a very calculated manner. He will get involved only when he knows he has the time to give it his sustained attention. Consequently, there are two distinctive (Rule of 72) habits of a Business Ambassador:

1) His willingness to say no, and
2) His persistent follow through when he says yes

Business Ambassador's thought processes consistently revolve around four concepts: Relationships, Momentum, Ambassador Equity, and Value. His involvement adds Value to everyone in his Embassy of relationships. He consistently creates Momentum through selectively chosen and meticulously maintained relationships. The end result is that his Ambassador Equity continually grows. There are many other practices that Business Ambassadors engage in. However, those four concepts are the driving Forces behind every Business Ambassador habit.

13

THE MYSTERY IN THE MATRIX

"Opportunities, many times, are so small that we glimpse them not, and yet they are often the seeds of great enterprises."
— Og Mandino

Many people are anxiously waiting for the great idea, the key contact, or the unique opportunity that will carry them onward to their next level of success. Every now and then something or someone will come their way and provide a burst of excitement. However, frequently nothing materializes, and they go back to watching for the next opportunity. In some ways, all of us are like hitch hikers with our thumbs out, looking for the ride that will take us to where we want to go. But the traffic is slow, and it seems as if there are few rides passing by the place we are standing. Some have been standing in the same place for a long time. And those rides that do pass by seem too preoccupied or too self-consumed to notice us.

I have tried to become a student of what a close friend of mine calls "walking slowly through the crowds." There are so many things to see and hear that most people miss. In fact, most of us walk through a crowd, (or in a general sense, walk through life), so fixated on where we want to go, what we need to accomplish, or when we need to be somewhere, that we are oblivious to our surroundings. It is a lot like a plow horse fitted with blinders that prevent the animal from being distracted by anything in his peripheral vision. Horses can see a lot more than most people realize. You can actually stand next to a horse's hind quarters, almost behind him, and he can see you just as clearly as if you were looking him square in the face. But those blinders limit his field of vision to a narrow tunnel.

To one degree or another, you might be like that person waiting and watching for the opportunity to hitch a ride. On the other hand, you might be like the person walking by with a blinder, so fixated on your own agenda that you are unaware of opportunities standing by with their thumbs out. Most of us, to some extent, are in one or both situations and not recognizing the opportunities all around us.

The Matrix of Relationship Momentum

People who can create their own Momentum and Ambassador Equity are those who realize that opportunities are everywhere. They don't have a scarcity mentality, even when everyone around them does. They look for an opportunity in everything and in every person, and usually they find it. Consequently, when they walk "slowly through the crowd," they see a very different world.

In the 1999 science-fiction movie, *The Matrix*, the hero, Neo, was destined to be the savior of the human race. However, to unlock the secrets that would empower him to defeat the bad guys, Neo had to understand the Matrix; that which he perceived as reality was actually a computer generated illusion. Once Neo saw the grid for what it was, he found that he could use that knowledge to manipulate it, generating the Force he needed to accomplish his mission to save the world.

A matrix in mathematics is simply a grid of numbers in rows and columns, each number being a function of other numbers in that grid. All elements within the system are dependent upon one another.

Imagine walking into an environment — a cocktail party, a coffee shop, or a company. While most see the setting as people moving, talking, or sitting alone, you see a complex array of gears and sprockets representing real and potential relationships among all those present. The machinery is far too complex for anyone to completely understand. But simply because you see it, you understand the tremendous Potential Energy present in every person in every crowd.

Believing and Caring

There are two primary characteristics of individuals who are able see the matrix of opportunities that underlies every crowd. One characteristic is believing and the other is caring. The first step in seeing the Matrix is believing that you are only one person away from unlocking Momentum for yourself, for someone within your sphere, or for someone with whom you come in contact. If you don't believe that the environment around you is swimming with possibilities, why look for them? You hear stories every now and then about the unexpected surprise that opened a door to success. But how many opportunities were missed because of the blinders or because of a preoccupation with doing business as usual?

Every time I enter a room or a network of people interconnected on even a casual level, immediately the matrix antenna goes up. Every person in that network has a story, a need, and a goal they are pursuing. Sometimes they boldly display those like walking billboards. Others are more subdued. But if you know the questions to ask and then truly listen to them, they begin to tell you who they are, where they're going, what they really want and need.

The second characteristic is caring. There are opportunities everywhere, most of them represented by a person. What keeps people from seeing and gaining access to that matrix is a tight fixation on their own needs. They care little for anything or anyone other than the people and opportunities that will promote their agenda. If people don't look like a key contact, they are never noticed.

Seeing every person as an opportunity takes both caring and a measure of faith because there is more than one kind of opportunity. If you are the kind of person who only recognizes people and needs that benefit you, then you will never figure out Relationship Momentum. Every person represents an opportunity, but sometimes that opportunity is for you to provide movement to another's endeavor. I am not naïve. I recognize when the other person is most likely to benefit monetarily from a relationship. Neither am I so quick to think I know the full potential of every interaction. One thing or one person can lead to another and to another and before you know it, you've been introduced to the key individual you would have never known any other way. That kind of thing happens to me all the time. You can either look specifically for something or someone who can fulfill a specific need, or you can dare to see the matrix for what it truly is, a system in which all elements are in a dependent relationship to one another. Ask yourself, are you looking for one person, casting away all other relationships, or are you looking for every person who could possibly help you or an Ambassador of yours move the needle?

The Hidden Gem

Much of my career has been in financial services, a world where people commonly display their power and influence. However, some of the most powerful are the ones who do not look the part.

One of the most economically significant clients that I have ever had was certainly the most inconspicuous prospect that anyone could think of. I met him at a dinner party filled with young execs that were hard at work sizing each other up, when I noticed a gentleman sitting at a table by himself. He was not wearing a suit and was actually out of dress code for the dinner club we were in. I decided to go over and introduce myself. He explained to me that he was in the city to see his nephew and they came to this particular gathering at the request of a local architectural firm. He started the conversation with the typical "ah shucks" style of a seemingly simple country boy. The conversation was not riveting, nor did I see an immediate opportunity to connect with him or to connect him with someone else. I began to tell him that I was a business Ambassador who specialized in Relationship Momentum and human capital. He then asked me a few questions. I explained my role further and then I turned the tables.

I asked him my "Five Questions of Commerce:"

1) What is your 1-3-5 year plan?

2) What is your Utopia and how do you get there?

3) What keeps you up at night?

4) Who do you want to meet?

5) What do you need yesterday? (Most people are too prideful to answer #2)

People love answering these questions. When the man began to answer, the matrix began to form around the room. Like the aforementioned Neo, I could see the connections forming and the branches of opportunity interfacing with my global sphere of influence. I found out that the man was not only a wealthy landowner, (50,000 acres of rich farmland on the Ohio River) but that he needed the services of at least ten people within my sphere (three of which had me on retainer).

We must learn to understand that there is a balance of giving and receiving, and to not prejudge the opportunities of a particular relationship. I try to contribute to others as the opportunity presents itself, often without any reasonable expectation of a return. You cannot treat people as merely a means to an end. You have to sincerely care for them — for their story, for their needs, and for their dreams. Concentrate on them as if they were the only person in the world. Everything else is insincerity, and most people will see through that pretty quickly. People who have the ability to see and access the dynamics of a relationship matrix are those with the ability to sincerely connect with each person they meet and then decipher the lines of connection that create commerce. Try it. Unlock the Matrix and watch a whole new world and a sub economy open up to you that you never thought possible.

14

THE EMBASSY OF COMMERCE

*"Commerce is a game of skill which everyone cannot play
and few can play well."*
— Ralph Waldo Emerson

The United States Foreign Commercial Service (USCS) is the trade promotion arm of the U.S. Department of Commerce's International Trade Administration. In addition to the USCS offices in 109 U.S. cities, there are 115 USCS centers located in the U.S. embassies and consulates of 70 countries around the world. The stated purpose of these centers is to support the export of American products and services through trade counseling, market intelligence, business matchmaking, advocacy, commercial diplomacy, and trade promotion programs. Over 85 percent of the companies assisted by the USCS are small and medium-sized businesses with fewer than 500 employees.

The USCS helped 18,500 companies facilitate 14,600 export successes worth more than $54 billion in fiscal year 2011 alone.

This is the same idea behind the local Chambers of Commerce, and, to some extent, they do the same thing. However, the existence of the USCS demonstrates that there are many more opportunities and commerce connections beyond the effective reach of local Chambers.

Imagine for a moment that your objective was to become an Ambassador presiding over a private version of such an Embassy. You would first need to construct a grand facility to house a similar commerce service. This Embassy of commerce would make key introductions, provide shortcuts to long-term economic relationships, and grant access to all kinds of business intelligence. Imagine CEOs, sales professionals, technical experts, and visionaries being continually drawn to your Embassy because of the mutual benefits they receive.

That vision is not as difficult to obtain as you might think. However, it does require a *metanoia* — a Greek word meaning, "a change in the way that you think."

Your first thought might be that you don't have the time or the capital to invest in establishing such an organization or constructing such an elaborate building. That sense of limited ability is the first way you would have to change your thinking. Powerful entities housed by bricks and mortar are a thing of the past. In the new world of ecommerce, networking, and virtual companies, boardrooms have been abandoned for coffee shops, clubhouses, and hotel lobbies. Neither is there any need to set up an organization or an association with bylaws, officers, or a set of complex regulations to govern idea and referral sharing. Just as the Embassy is not housed in a building, the connections are not formed within the context of an organization, but by *mutually beneficial relationships.*

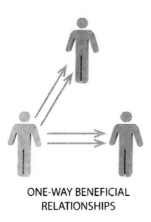

ONE-WAY BENEFICIAL
RELATIONSHIPS

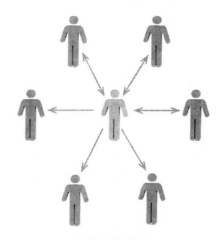

MUTALLY BENEFICIAL
RELATIONSHIPS

But how, you wonder, *can all of this happen without some catalyst or central organizing entity?* In this, your thinking is dead on. There must be some kind of attraction and some kind of glue to hold it all together. The *metanoia,* or new way of thinking, is that <u>you</u> are the catalyst and the central organizing entity. You are the senior diplomat, the Ambassador managing business relationships in such a way as to

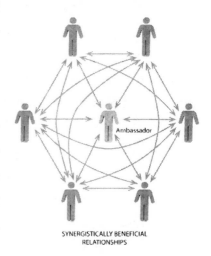

SYNERGISTICALLY BENEFICIAL
RELATIONSHIPS

create a virtual Embassy of commerce not unlike a personal version of the USCS. You must change your thought pattern into *becoming* commerce instead of always looking for it.

RELATIONSHIP MOMENTUM AND AMBASSADOR EQUITY

Ask yourself these questions:

Who is benefiting from my capital investments of money, knowledge, and influence?

From whom am I receiving those same benefits?

There is nothing new about business networks or lead-generation associations. But many of them never get beyond one-way or the occasional two-way relationship.

A key element to the ongoing success of your Embassy of commerce is the entry fee. The price of admission is that each person has to take on the role of an Ambassador. They must be committed to establishing and maintaining relationships, not only for personal benefits but also for the benefits to all others, as opportunities present themselves. The number, strength, and frequency of these mutually beneficial relationships establishes the intrinsic Value of your Embassy of Commerce. That is what I call *Ambassador Equity*. It is the Mass of your deposits and the size of your Ambassador sphere.

This is where the concepts of Relationship Momentum and Ambassador Equity begin to have a significant impact on your strategic objectives. Newton's First Law of Motion states that bodies at rest tend to stay at rest while bodies in Motion tend to stay in Motion. Their Momentum (or lack thereof) remains the same, until they are acted upon — by an *external Force*. For an object in Motion, that redirecting Force could be some kind of Drag, such as Gravity. When an object achieves a certain Velocity (Escape Velocity), it has the ability to escape the Drag of the earth's gravitational pull and thus continue on its path, propelled only by its own Momentum.

One-way relationships are actually a Drag on your progress, draining time, money, and energy from your Momentum. Even if you are the one who happens to be benefiting, that one-way relationship will never produce an Embassy of commerce. Over the long haul, givers are not attracted to takers. One-way relationships do not attract other Ambassador types, generate Ambassador Equity, or create synergistic Relationship Momentum.

Two-way relationships are better in that they benefit others and yourself. However, in a network of synergistic relationships where all parties benefit from all other parties, the power of Relationship Momentum begins to take over. Like a nuclear fission, once it gets started, it has the potential to expand very rapidly without any additional effort of your own.

SHADOW EQUITY – VOLUME WITHOUT MASS

It is common for people to simply appear to have Ambassador Equity, when all they really have is a large stack of business cards collected over the years. I call it Shadow Equity — the appearance of power, influence, and wealth with little real substance. In physical terms — it is Volume without Mass. This is evidenced by the fact that they can drop a lot of names, but don't have the Ambassador Equity to get anything done, or the ability to actually provide any real help to you.

Everyone knows that business relationships are essential to success. But all relationships are not equal. Don't be fooled into thinking that the factors contributing to success are simply the number of business relationships or even the influence of the people in your relationship network. You could have hundreds of relationships with very powerful people with none of them contributing to the improvement of your Relationship Momentum.

In many cases, the continual effort to build relationships with powerful, influential people has a *negative* effect. Because those relationships never progress beyond a one-way type, the pursuit of what they consider to be these "strategic relationships" becomes a waste of time and energy — that is, a Drag on the Momentum toward their strategic objectives.

Here is the point that so many people miss because it doesn't make sense without a new way of thinking. An Embassy of commerce filled with common people in synergistically beneficial relationships will create far more Relationship Momentum than typical business associations with scores of the rich and powerful. Ambassador Equity that contributes to Relationship Momentum has much more to do with the nature and management of your relationships than it does with those people's perceived influence.

15

THE AMBASSADOR COUNCIL

"If you want to go fast, go alone. If you want to
go far, go with others."
— African Proverb

I have always been in the business of prospecting. I've prospected for consulting clients, for employees, for new ideas, for funding, and for human capital. I sat down one day and realized that I was always on the hunt, as if my next paycheck depended on it. Eventually I grew tired of the monotonous hunt and decided to plant something that I could cultivate. I was a lot like a prehistoric Neanderthal making the transition from a hunter-gatherer to a cultivation-based subsistence. The hunter-gatherers mostly died out. The cultivators survived and prospered.

My ideas and initiatives needed more strategic movement than I could supply on my own. So, I created what I now call an Ambassador Council. This should not be confused with a networking club, study group, personal board of directors, or even a consortium that gets together to talk about creating new business. I formed the Ambassador Council with the idea of establishing measurable and repeatable opportunities that result in commerce. Like a Neanderthal, I discovered that a cultivated crop grew every day, while hunting required my active participation.

Networking groups are full of Nominators. A Nominator is someone willing to give you peripheral referrals. There is certainly nothing wrong with someone giving you names and business cards that may or may not lead to a new client. But nominator relationships are usually one-way affairs, and the unions are only skin deep. Just like people, every project, product, or purpose needs relationships that are built on trust, effective communication, and are maintained over time. That goes much deeper than the exchange of businesses cards. Our ideas and initiatives need relationships with real, live Ambassadors. In order to create a clear contrast and distinction, below are some of the characteristics of Nominators and Ambassadors.

Nominators:

- Are familiar with your story
- Are willing to occasionally tell others about you
- Occasionally provide leads
- Have very little emotional and often no economic ties to your initiative

Ambassadors:

- Know your story intimately. They can recite your elevator speech, your Ethos, and your Value Proposition within a moment's notice.
- Have the authority to speak on your behalf to evangelize the story
- Bring commerce to your door step

- Have either an emotional and/or economic tie to your initiative

I have had plenty of Nominators, and I am very thankful for them. However, what I needed most was someone to make my interests their own. But why would anyone want to do that? Isn't capitalism built upon self-interest? Once again, I had to change the way I thought about the dynamics of commerce.

The First Council

Dr. Stephanie Hancock is a bestselling author and a close friend of mine. She is also the niece of King Emmanuel Adebayo, the traditional ruler of the Emure Kingdom, a province of Nigeria with a population of nearly one million. The King was crowned in 2008 when he retired from his position as Police Chief of Lagos, Nigeria. King Emmanuel has a vision of peace, unity, and progress in a country known for its corruption and infighting, and by the grace of God, I was able to go there and help make a difference.

Dr. Hancock was putting together a team of consultants to come to Nigeria at the invitation of the Adassa Foundation. When I heard the King's story, I was compelled to accept the invitation.

The foundation brought me in to meet with the King's Chieftains and business leaders, and to teach them about Relationship Momentum. I began by introducing the idea of an abundance mentality and the concept of working together. Instead of seeing every other business owner as a competitor and an enemy, I explained how they could all win together. From a global, national, and even local perspective, commerce is not a zero-sum game. That is, one business doesn't necessarily have to lose in order for another to win. An Ambassador Council requires that kind of approach.

The meetings were a success and after subsequent trips and trainings, we formed the first Ambassador Council in the country. We were even able to bring together a group of business owners who, along with the King, would ultimately fund the establishment and growth of more than twenty new businesses in Emure Kingdom.

Forming the Council

The Ambassador Council is basically an incubator for Ambassador Equity and Relationship Momentum. It can be within a business or corporation. It can exist within an industry or can be organized geographically. Whatever the scope, the Council must be made up of like-minded people in search of the same thing. It can be formed with any group who needs Momentum on a product, project, or purpose. The Council can be small or large and can meet as often as is relevant.

An Ambassador Council must maintain Momentum in and of itself. The sequence of the gatherings may last for years or only a short time. However, the potential is for relationships that are accretive and that can for last decades. I have created Ambassador Councils with CEOs, salesmen, pastors, recruiters, and even lawyers. The goal is growth and the Ambassador Equity gained is almost always in the form of human capital.

I put together an Ambassador Council of Financial Services Sales Managers who were in need of two kinds of Human Capital. They needed new clients for their advisors and new financial advisors in general. As was the case when I began working with the business owners in Nigeria, some of the managers did not enthusiastically embrace the concept. They looked at the other potential Council members as the competition, and consequently, did not want to share "their slice of cake."

What they found was that there were several differences in the profile of the potential member. The result of the Council was the ability to capture Human Capital that would normally be lost. They did this by sending their leads, relationships, and introductions that were not a perfect fit to someone who had a higher likelihood of closing the opportunity. The members found that every prospect could become a future win for someone in the Council. That success would, in turn, become a deposit of Equity that would ultimately work its way back to the source. This practice changed the careers of many people involved in that Ambassador Council. Imagine the Momentum of your meetings and the evaporation of opportunity cost, when almost everyone you meet could be a lucrative opportunity to someone in your Council and accretive to your own acquisition of Ambassador Equity.

There are only a few rules to forming a council:

1) The members of the Council must be very good at what they do. You cannot afford issues of Brand or Value hurting the ability for all to profit from the Council.

2) There must be individual goals set that the Council works together to accomplish.

3) There must be an account of the activity, commerce, and successes that are a result of the Council. This will help with the Council's Momentum in and of itself.

4) Each individual Brand, Ethos, and Value Proposition must be intimately known by each of the other members.

5) Whether it is weekly, monthly or quarterly, the Council meetings must be strategic in nature and in sequence.

6) You have to have fun. The members must enjoy one another. The key component to the Momentum of the Council is the fact that the relationships are built on more than just the economic opportunities at hand.

Members of a Council certainly do not have to be in the same industry. They just need to have the heart and mind to work collaboratively. A council works the same whether it is a group of restaurant owners, contractors or CEOs of Fortune 100 companies. Ambassador Councils are made up of Relationships that are both emotional and economic. Together they can generate much needed Momentum for any product, project, or purpose.

The Council is not necessarily the place for all of your Ambassadors. The Council is merely a way to place a strategic model around the commerce that can be harnessed through the power of a close knit group. There have been many things in my life that have contributed to dramatic and long-lasting change. Discovering the power of Ambassador Equity and the potential of the Ambassador Council has been one of the most significant, to the point that every idea and initiative I engage with will have its own an Ambassador Council. I hope yours will too.

16
FOREST FOR THE TREES

"The Main Thing is to keep The Main Thing The Main Thing."
— Stephen Covey

Pat McRae was formerly a U.S. Diplomat with the U.S. & Foreign Commercial Service and responsible for opening international markets to U.S. products and services. Pat led a team of trade specialists (or as I would call them) Business Ambassadors. He described to me one day how his department created commerce on a global scale.

Pat gave an example of an entrepreneur in North Carolina who manufactured cigar cutters. The manufacturer approached the U.S. Commercial Service Export Assistance Center (USEAC) and expressed interest in exporting his product. The USEAC assisted with research on the international sales and distribution of cigar cutters. The synopsis came back with a list of target markets. The USEAC made connections with the U.S. Embassies abroad, and they then put together an export strategy. This may have included potential joint venture partners, distribution, logistics, etc. In short, there was a definitive system in place to connect the dots for a product to enter the global markets.

The matrix for foreign commerce and trade can be complex if you are not used to working in that environment. However, Pat describes the complexities of international trade as if it was as simple as selling lemonade from the street corner. It seemed easy to Pat only because he has spent most of his professional life opening foreign markets for U.S. firms and as a Diplomat with the power to make things happen internationally. His cohorts made it possible for products and services to enter the marketplace by brokering human capital, relationships, and awareness. Pat was and still is an expert in creating Ambassador Equity and sustaining Relationship Momentum on a global scale.

Commerce in our local markets works in a similar fashion, but without the import-export framework of the U.S. government. Locally, the relationships, introductions, promotion, and Momentum are the responsibility of individual entrepreneurs. As a result, there are many more misses than hits. The reason for the absence of success is that there is usually no true liaison or commerce proponent (Ambassador) to help create the Motion needed to move the product, project, or purpose forward.

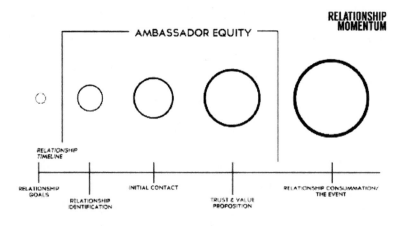

The 4 Acquisitions

The single most important thing that I want to impart in this book is the concept of Ambassador Equity — the need to have third-party Ambassadors telling your story and driving Relationship Momentum. Ambassador Equity can be accumulated in many ways. The four most common I have described in this manuscript are listed below:

1) Acquiring the prestige of the Business Ambassador to tell the story and to circulate pivotal relationships
2) Acquiring the influence of an Embassy of Commerce to create your own human capital exchange
3) Acquiring the power of the crowd through social media
4) Acquiring Osmosis Growth through the expanded reach of your own Ambassador Council(s)

Product, projects, or purposes gain Mass and Velocity through any one of these four types of Ambassador Equity. Imagine if you were able to apply all of them. Ambassador Equity reaches its intended Mass when all four of these acquisitions are being implemented effectively. The result is the kind of Relationship Momentum necessary to create and sustain a successful career or venture.

PART 3
V_s

Strategic Velocity

1
STRATEGIC VELOCITY

*"You may not be interested in strategy, but
strategy is interested in you."*
— Leon Trotsky

In physics, Velocity is known as an object's rate of change with respect
to its location. Velocity is not the same thing as speed. Speed is very
important when it comes to the time-value of money, bandwidth,
profits, and costs. The problem with using speed as a measure of
progress is that it only tells you the rate of movement. Velocity is a
measure of both direction and rate of movement.

Let's reexamine the relationships within the science of Relationship
Momentum. It is not sufficient to focus solely on the Mass of the
Three Equities (Brand, Value, and Ambassador) or the rate at which
each move.

The Relationship Momentum equation is:

$$Rm=E^3V_s$$

First of all, it's important to note that anything multiplied by zero equals zero. If any of those individual Equities (E^3) equals zero, your Relationship Momentum will also equal zero.

Secondly, the final element and component to our equation is as important as the first. If you are moving fast, even in a consistent direction, you may not be moving towards your intended goals. Strategic Velocity (V_s) is the rate of movement of the combined Equities in a direction that most efficiently accomplishes the strategic objectives. The consequence is that you must think before, during, and after you move.

Football Physics

In my younger days, I spent some time as a college football coach. I remember one particular young man who possessed a tremendous amount of raw talent. However, the young linebacker was rarely successful due to his timing and angles. He never seemed to be at the right place at the right time. The angles of pursuit, reading, and reacting to defenses have far more impact on team success than simply being bigger, faster, and stronger. Occasionally, he would create a disturbance in the opposing team's game plan or make jaw-dropping plays. The young man could have been a great player if we could just arrange for the other team to simply run each play right at him. But opponents figured out pretty quickly that was not their best option. The young man was a great physical specimen and had the heart of a lion, but his limitations regarding the broader spectrum of required skills made him a liability. As a result, he could not contribute significantly to the overall team strategy.

I am sure that most of us have worked with people like this. They have a ton of talent and their work ethic is never called into question. The issue arises when they sacrifice strategy for strength and speed. Who cares how fast you get "there" if you do not know where "there" is?

A Ticket to Springfield

A friend and nationally renowned speaker, Don Connelly, once told me a story of a man who was concerned about his business ventures in Springfield. He went to the Amtrak station to buy a train ticket. However, when the attendant asked the man whether he wanted a ticket to Springfield, Ohio, Tennessee, North Carolina, or Kentucky, the man simply replied, "Whichever one will get me there the fastest!"

Many people in the world of business relationships are like the man buying a train ticket to Springfield. They are not so particular about which Springfield (or definition of success) they are pursuing, only which one is the quickest and easiest to attain. Those who do not take the time to specify their destination or define their particular definition of success will often waste their talents on trips to places they do not want to go.

Groupon Speed

Consider the Groupon phenomena as an example. I cannot recall another company or concept moving faster and acquiring more Ambassador Equity than Groupon. In 2008, Andrew Mason founded the tech startup out of an existing company. He then set out to create a viral marketplace for those seeking to harness "the power of the crowd" for consumer discounts. What he and his team created was a source of Momentum for social couponing. Groupon quickly became a staple in the daily lives of consumers and retailers alike. In three short years, the company rose from its humble beginnings to a social media giant that eventually turned down a $6 Billion dollar offer from the search-engine behemoth Google.

Groupon not only gained speed and Velocity through Ambassador Equity, they were able to accomplish what few other products or companies have. They rewarded each Groupon Ambassador in the form of discounts. Not just a handful of select individuals but EVERY ONE OF THEM! The two most powerful elements needed for viral growth, Ambassadors and Economic Relationships, were being created simultaneously through Andrew Mason's Groupon business model.

Talk about Relationship Momentum! They had a great Brand and Ethos, a fantastic Value Proposition, and all the Ambassador Equity in the world. So what went wrong?

Groupon was moving too fast and, at times, in the wrong direction. It was quite possibly the fastest growing company in history. What led to many of their problems and could ultimately spell their demise was a mistake made in the initial launch phase of the company. To harness the power of the consumer, one must have something to consume. Groupon knew that they would create raving fans for their site and service, but what they were not able to do, was create raving fans of their retail partners. Though they were able to provide significant discounts for the masses, unless the newly acquired traffic for the retailers turned into repeat business, the relationship between the business owners and Groupon could not create sustainable Momentum. Retailers offer discounts to attract first-time customers with the hope of making them repeat customers or of creating additional point-of-purchase sales. However, if new Groupon customers represent one-time customers who only purchase the discounted item, then the business model is far less attractive to retailers. It was no longer a win-win arrangement. The inability to create a sustainable a flow of repeat customers ultimately diminished Groupon's Value Proposition. It's a perfect example of simply moving too fast and lacking a few strategic guardrails that could have prevented the problems.

Groupon grew into a colossal organization with more than 10,000 employees virtually overnight. It was not that the founders of Groupon did not want to repair their foundational problems, it was that they couldn't. The company was too big, was moving too fast, and was making too much money to change its course.

Velocity is speed in a given direction. However, Strategic Velocity is the optimum speed in the optimum direction to accomplish the strategic objectives.

There have been other companies and products that have suffered the same problems as Groupon. They grew so quickly that they could not sustain the promised Value Proposition, and they were moving too fast to change the business model. It is one thing to be built for speed, but another to be built to last.

2
TRUE NORTH

"Don't become a mere recorder of facts, but try to penetrate the mystery of their origin."
— Ivan Pavlov

Whenever you embark on a journey, there are two things you need to determine. You need to figure out precisely where you are, and its relevance to your final destination. Navigators call it True North. Those two little pieces of data become the context of your entire adventure. When I talk about pinpointing your locations, I am speaking metaphorically. Where are you in your career, product development, and personal growth; in your education, skills and experience? Where are you in your business development? What relationships are adding to or eroding your Momentum? Before launching a new idea, you need to take inventory. A SWOT analysis is a great tool to guide that process. Some go through that kind of internal evaluation as regularly as a check up with their doctor, identifying their Strengths, Weaknesses, Opportunities, and Threats. Without that step, planning a journey is like calculating your direction without knowing your starting point. Where you wind up is a matter of random chance.

The second requirement for your expedition is securing a good compass that enables you to determine which way is North. Every compass bearing is relative to True North or what you have determined to be the proverbial "promised land" for your initiative. An objective that is along the path to success should always be measured in its relation to the prize!

I could not imagine creating a plan or deriving strategy without first knowing where I was. That requires an honest evaluation of the assets or liabilities I have at my disposal. Only then do I develop a plan for where I want to go. Everything else I do from that point onward should be in reference to that inventory and my picture of success. Elements of that inventory may change from decade to decade, year to year, or even quarter to quarter. Although your business will grow and evolve, your destination rarely changes. Think about that picture often — so often that you are able to communicate and even illustrate it for others. The practice of making the vision transferable and communicable is a key factor in developing internal and external Ambassadors. It will also shape your Brand Ethos and help you stay true to your Value Proposition

Just the Beginning

Ideas don't stop with success. In fact, success enables you to be more creative than ever because the ideas are easier to fund. Consequently, I have only begun to ideate. The important part of building upon proven ideas is that you do not allow your picture of success to change without serious contemplation and self-evaluation. Many successful people and products have lost their bearing and damage the picture by carelessly building on the foundation of previous success. New Coke anyone?

It often makes sense for you to pause and take inventory of your current relationships in their entirety and not just with respect to an idea or initiative. How many Ambassadors do you have? Do they understand and support your picture of success? Are they headed to a destination where you wish to go? Can they contribute to your Relationship Momentum? What relationships are emotional, economic, or merely tactical? In the search for Relationship Momentum, it is very important to establish your current ecosystem before building upon it.

That being said, the next time I come upon a new idea that I feel is worth advancing, I would first sit down and figure out where I am (take inventory) and where I want to go (my picture of success). How consistent is this new idea with the overall picture and general direction of my life and career? If it advances the direction and intensifies the picture, I then establish what I consider to be the milestones and timelines required for the journey. I then apply every objective to the Relationship Momentum equation to make sure that I am moving in step with True North (my picture of success).

Winner Takes All

There is such a thing as relative success. This is the type of success most people have experience with. People are often perfectly content with getting close to their goals and dreams. However, there are those few individuals, projects, or companies that have strategic objectives and a True North focused on winner-takes-all propositions. In such a case, there is no such thing as relative success. You win or lose, hit the bull's eye or miss the target. This would be the case in combat, in political campaigns, or closing the deal in a sales presentation. I've never been in combat and never run for public office. I have, however, closed the sale, reached the event, and led the acquisition of several companies. I understand the razor's edge between success and failure. I have tried to make it a habit to place myself in more "Winner Takes All" scenarios, as it keeps me focused and relentlessly committed to the cause. It has been my experience that many people experience relative success as opposed to reaching their dreams because they never had a true picture of what they were after. They did not visualize it, write it down, and in turn, help others to see it as well.

That scenario may be very rare in the scope of one's entire life. An individual can go on to be relatively successful after having lost an election or a big sale. However, in the context of an immediate opportunity, it may be a winner-takes-all event. Or the strategic significance of the circumstances may represent a once-in-a-lifetime opportunity, essential to accomplishing a company's Vision Statement or an individual's lifetime objective. It is hard to know how often opportunities will present themselves, but in those critical moments, you cannot afford to miscalculate by using the wrong set of metrics or by not knowing your definition of success, your True North.

3

MAY THE FORCE BE WITH YOU

"Strategy without tactics is the slowest way to victory.
Tactics without strategy is the noise before defeat."
— Sun Tzu (*The Art of War*)

As a young businessman, I initiated many projects that eventually ran off the rails. Most of them were due to a lack of planning or pause when a change was needed. I often did not understand the tactics I needed to employ until it was too late. I have learned a lot over the years, and most of the lessons were hard ones. Consequently, I have been forced to pay my fair share of "stupid tax." Today, I am a better man and a stronger entrepreneur for it.

"To tack" in sailing terminology means to make strategic turns in order to capture the most efficient use of the available energy. From it we get the word "tactic." When you are trying to create Momentum in a business environment that depends on external Forces, sometimes a straight line is not the most efficient course. When sailing against a headwind, you are often required to zig zag, looking for the most efficient tack.

Depending on an external Force rather than simply aiming and firing at your goal might seem to suggest a new model to gauge your success. But in actuality, the dynamics of progress toward your strategic objectives are still measured and monitored in terms of physical movement. The physics of sailing simply describe a business environment in which you are almost completely dependent on the external Forces for movement. Consequently, progress toward your goals is all about how well you foresee your tack, execute your turn, and trim your sails.

A note about strategy and tactics: your strategic objective is always a single direction. It is a vector that points to where you want to end up. A tack or tactic will often veer off temporarily into another direction in order to catch a prevailing wind. For instance, you goal is to provide advice for a fee to potential investors. Veering off to obtain a master's degree in financial planning is your tack. Though it may be a longer distance to travel, that tack is nonetheless the most efficient course.

The problem emerges when people don't understand the difference between strategic objectives and short-term tactical responses. For example, they tack to the northeast, and as a result, increase their Velocity. They begin selling term-life insurance to pay for the added tuition costs, which picks up speed and turns into a pretty good business. But instead of tacking back toward their strategic end goal, they just continue on the same course. In other words, they interpret speed as success toward their objective when they are, in fact, only moving farther and farther off course.

One of my primary mistakes was measuring my current success simply by the speed of my project. I would get excited when things began to move quickly. However, I was like a person looking for a breeze and allowing it to take me wherever it would go.

The second false indicator was the number of people who were getting involved. Since I am a relational guy, I tended to look at the number of people signing on and say, "Ah ha, we are getting somewhere." I have learned that this is neither a certain measure of strategic success nor of Momentum.

THE MOST EFFICIENT TACK

Turning is simply the tactical application of Force. As I have explained in a previous chapter, the larger the vessel, the harder it is to turn it. This is also the case with speed. The faster you go, the harder it is to change direction. Consequently, you have to learn how to apply resistance in order make course corrections with optimum efficiency.

There are three ways to make tactical course corrections by applying Force. I will illustrate with examples of paddling a canoe.

Pull or ADDED FORCE — If you want a canoe to veer to the left, paddle on the right. This is a positive application of Force and the most efficient way to turn. This corresponds to tactical changes you make, not by abandoning what you have been doing, but by simply adding more energy to something you are already doing. Paddle harder on the right. It is, however, the slowest way to turn.

Push or OPPOSING FORCE — To execute the quickest possible turn, you apply resistance on one side. Paddle backwards on the left, and the canoe makes a sudden left turn. In terms of canoe speed and Momentum, this is the least efficient way to turn. You have executed the turn by slamming on the brakes with regard to a particular initiative. This tactic corresponds to an abandonment of a current program or objective. Opposing Force turns are often the result of the lack of foresight or planning.

Point or ADDED LATERAL FORCE — In canoeing terminology this is called a j-stroke. At the end of the stroke, the paddler rotates his paddle and pushes out and away from the canoe. The result is Force applied laterally that changes the direction. In terms of loss of speed and Momentum, it is somewhere between push and pull. You change course quickly, but not as inefficiently as paddling backward on one side. This corresponds to a situation in which you are able to change course without the loss of Momentum.

Of the three ways to apply Force, the most common tactic is push because is it produces an immediate response. Perhaps, the need is for the quickest turn you can execute. This is how we often make the most mistakes. What we learn from applying the Laws of Motion to success is that executing a turn by applying opposing Force is the greatest Momentum killer and the least efficient tact. The trick is to make changes without dissipating your forward movement.

Think about this concept as it correlates to Relationship Momentum. We often build relationships with a potential buyer, manager, or client, and the moment that we begin to feel the least bit of Drag (resistance), we slam on the breaks. We react emotionally and this often impedes Momentum greatly. The challenge is to take a step back and react strategically with applied Force to assess and turn, all the while keeping in mind what the end result (the direction) is desired to be. The application of strategic Force is an imperative component to success with your product, project or purpose. The afore mentioned "stupid tax" can be very beneficial if you learn from it; but, like my father said about my first marriage, "you got a good education, son, you just paid a lot for it."

4
DERAILED

"The essential thing in heaven and earth . . . is that there should be a long obedience in the same direction. This has always resulted, in the long run, in something which has made life worth living."
— Friedrich Nietzsche

I once took a personality test designed to create my own psychological profile. The idea was to identify my strengths and weaknesses as the Chief Executive Officer of the company. Back then I called them potential pathways or potential derailers of success. Today I think of those qualities in terms of movement — the potential for Momentum or the potential for Drag. A question arises: which is a more effective means of increasing Velocity and Momentum? Should we pedal harder or grease the wheel bearings; create a more streamlined business design or increase horsepower?

The quick answer is, of course, to do a little of both. Increase efficiency and reduce Drag (i.e., the things that tend to derail your progress). This is generally true, but still requires a closer look.

There is usually both a "stop doing" and "start doing" list associated with personal growth and development as a business leader. The same is true for entrepreneurs, husbands, wives, and cause advocates. The positive habits we need to develop often correspond to a list of counter-habits we need to break or extinguish. Both good and bad habits have significant impact on Relationship Momentum. However, the impact is often very different. Think of it in terms of a bank account. You can invest in a valuable relationship for many years in order to build up a great amount of Equity (an essential element of Relationship Momentum). But you can destroy that relationship and decades of accumulated Equity in a moment of time with a single act or an ongoing bad habit. That is true with unfaithfulness in marriage, dishonesty in business, or the lack of self-control in management. Though you may have built up a positive balance in that account, with a single act or a series of acts, you bankrupt the relationship almost instantly.

If by the grace and forgiveness of your friends, family, customers, or business partners, they give you another chance, it can still take many years to restore trust in those relationships (i.e. restore Equity in those accounts). Even when the grace and forgiveness come from God, you normally pay a price for those bad habits and decisions. Even when God gives you a clean slate, starting over has a huge impact on Relationship Momentum. We all know that life's greatest blessings and benefits are the result of long-term, uninterrupted faithfulness to people and to principles. God and people may give you grace to starting over again, but it is difficult to build Relationship Equity and Momentum when you have to repeatedly start from scratch. Consequently, a "stop-doing" or "don't-ever-do" list has far more potential impact on Relationship Momentum than a "start-doing" list.

DON'T-DO LIST

There are many elements that can contribute to positive movement. That is the primary focus of this little book. To tell the whole story, however, I have listed seven common elements that can create Drag, if not completely derail a project, a career, or a relationship.

1. A Scarcity Mentality

A scarcity mentality develops over a long period of time, often from childhood. This frame of reference resides in individuals because of their circumstance or early relationships. They have become so scripted in scarcity mentality, it is difficult for them to develop any kind of Personal Momentum. They are like those who drive with their foot on the brake because they have a hard time getting beyond their fear or their scarcity expectations. This way of thinking hinders many people, particularly salesmen, fundraisers, and cause proponents. It is very hard for them to imagine that people actually will want to buy, give, or volunteer.

Personal Momentum is synonymous with optimism and faith. There are those who have somehow flipped the switch on their previous experiences and have used scarcity as the driving Force to create Momentum in their lives. My father has provided a life-long example of reaching back to help others. His influence is precisely why I served for years as Chairman of the Board for an after-school program serving at-risk inner-city youth. What my dad and I have discovered is that once a switch is flipped in a young man or young woman, then and only then, are all things possible for their lives.

2. Narcissistic Approach to Relationships

This is another form of scarcity mentality. The fable of the boy and the figs goes back as far as the Greek Stoic philosopher, Epictetus (AD 55 – AD 135). In its earliest version, a boy puts his hand into a pitcher of figs and grasps so many that he cannot withdraw his fist through the narrow opening. When he bursts into tears out of frustration, "an honest fellow" who stood by advises him to take only half the figs. He would then be free. However, the boy refuses to let go. The moral of the story is that in order to get what we want, we have to be willing to give back.

Some people are persistent takers, grasping for every benefit that can be wrung out of that relationship. That is true of business, social, and even marriage relationships. Whether the source is greed, fear, or simply a game to play, being a persistent taker derails Relationship Momentum. No doubt, you can create movement by being a taker, but certainly not Relationship Momentum. The only people you attract to yourself are other persistent takers, who at the first opportunity will take everything you have. Rather than promoting your cause, all your so-called trusted Ambassadors are simply lying in wait to derail your Relationship Momentum by an ambush.

3. Careless Words

There are so many ways for good intentions to get lost in translation. Communication breakdowns frequently occur when too much is said, information and opinions are not guarded, and when email is involved. It is not a good practice to walk around your relationships on eggshells, but it is a healthy habit to think before you speak, as you type, and especially before you hit the "Send" button. The "cc:" and particularly the "bcc:" functions enable you with one keystroke to copy or blind copy anyone and everyone on your contacts list. However, what is done in the guise of keeping someone in the loop, is often motivated by our dark side — a way of ensuring that everyone knows who should get credit (especially if it is you) or blame (especially if it makes you look better by comparison). Remember, you need to be very careful what you say when you are angry. And you need to be ten times more careful when you put it into writing. A written communiqué documents your momentary emotion as if it was your perpetual state of mind.

4. Different Standards of Follow-Through

How contentious are you about following through on your commitments? There are a lot of people who, for various reasons, have a casual approach to time, financial, and service accountability. Some of those reasons are attributed to forgetfulness, time, and financial budgeting (no margin), or the lack of prioritization. However, it doesn't matter how you justify the lack of follow-through — your most important clients, donors, and customers will probably follow suit. They didn't get to be important by following those habits. In fact, if they are successful themselves, they most likely think of time as money. In other words, they have the habit of converting the loss of time and effort to dollars as if they are billing you for the time. This habit is so embedded, that most can't turn it off. They see tardiness as the Value you place on them and their time. They see your lack of promptness and forgetfulness as a sign of disorganization or worse — self-importance. If they have to follow up on your performance when you should have taken the initiative to keep them informed, they see you as a person who complicates their life. This unaccountability can easily derail trust in your habits if not your character. Think of margin (surplus time and money) as Equity. The margin you create in your schedule and budget to ensure on-time performance is a form of Equity that contributes to Relationship Momentum.

5. Unclear, Mismanaged Expectations

In every relationship, it is very important for all parties to have a clear understanding of the intrinsic Value to each person. Just as there is no such thing as a perpetual motion machine, all ongoing relationships require investments of time, effort, and energy, particularly the ones that are powerful enough to generate significant Momentum.

Everyone creates an expectation of what the return on investment (ROI) will be. The problem is that many contractual relationships begin with a lot of unqualified expectations. When relations derail over unclear expectations, it is often because of two extreme applications of the agreement.

At one extreme, companies create insanely long contracts with very small print that spell out in detail the terms of the agreement. Some of this is necessary because of regulations and liability. The terms of that small print become relevant in only the rarest situations. Those kinds of agreements seldom derail relationships. Usually, these generally benign contracts are the ones you must confirm to gain Internet access or to load computer software.

The notorious derailers are characterized by telecommunications agreements (cell phone, internet, and cable television). With these agreements the true cost never turns out to be anything close to the advertized price. It doesn't take many experiences arguing with customer service representatives to develop the opinion that everything about the Value Proposition of these agreements is constructed as a misrepresentation that deceives rather than defines the relationship. Creating expectations in a relationship that you cannot or have no intention of fulfilling is the prime definition of defrauding.

The other application of agreements that tends to derail relationships is the vague handshake. Though people pine for the days when deals were sealed with a handshake, that memory represents a much simpler world. Handshakes notwithstanding, people who make agreements verbally or who do not outline expectations specifically, run the risk of seeing relationships derail. Wise businesspersons use written agreements, not because they do not trust their business partners, but in order to guard the relationship from being derailed over misunderstood or misremembered expectations.

6. The Law of Diminishing Returns on Relationships

The law of diminishing return simply states that increased levels of investment (of time, energy, or resources) will result in increased levels of return — but up to a point. Eventually, the curve that charts the rate of return-on-investment flattens out. As the curve flattens, your rate of return decreases. In some application of the law, the curve goes negative. In other words, greater and greater investments will eventually result in an overall loss. For example, a positive return-on-investment in a particular asset class for a portion of your portfolio might result in a terrible loss if you put everything you had in that investment.

In terms of Relationship Momentum, the more your serve, support, and invest in a relationship, the greater the return on your investment, up to a point. At the same time, the greater number of relationships and Ambassadors you have will help you create more Momentum, but also only up to a point. A steady balance of diversification with attention to bandwidth is imperative.

7. Lack of Evolving Value

I wrote previously about this as a potential relationship derailer. Simply restated, customers and clients grow accustomed to a certain level of Value, whether it is the Value of a service, a product, or a relationship. If the Value of the relationship does not evolve, both parties begin to take the other for granted. The result is that those on the receiving end of the Value Proposition begin to shop around. Eventually, the relationship is derailed.

THESE ARE JUST A FEW examples of things on a "don't-do" list that can have an enormous impact on high-potential relationships. I assure you there are many more. In a general sense, you can identify other derailing forces by thinking in terms of protecting the Equity that you are investing into that relationship.

5
THE BIG BOARD

"It's a lack of clarity that creates chaos and frustration.
Those emotions are poisonous to any living goal."
— Steve Maraboli

In my career I have often struggled with an overwhelming sense of chaos and disorder. I have engaged with current relationships, searched for new ones, and filtered though invitations to Ambassador other people's ideas. Despite my organizational shortcomings, I had success early on, but my distractions and inability to focus (especially in times of great stress) put a hard limit on what I could accomplish. With so many opportunities for projects and relationships knocking at the door, I almost began to wish that they would all go away. What should be a great blessing began to feel a lot like a curse.

My attitude changed several years ago, when I was introduced to a good friend who was able to reach into my chaotic world and provide me with a moment of peace and pause. His approach to helping me was not to turn me into a champion of details. Instead, he helped me systematize and manage my attention. In other words, he helped me focus on what was really important, when and only when it was really important to do so. He introduced me to the concept of "dashboarding."

CFIT — Controlled Flight Into Terrain

The 1972 crash of Eastern Airlines Flight 401 is the classic example of Controlled Flight into Terrain (CFIT), an aviation term used to describe a perfectly airworthy aircraft under complete pilot control being inadvertently flown into the ground. When Flight 401 approached Miami International Airport, a defective indicator light failed to illuminate and signify that the nose gear was locked into the down position. Three experienced and highly qualified pilots became so fixated on the landing gear light that no one noticed the autopilot disengage at 2,000 feet. By the time they realized what was happening, it was too late. Since that accident, all airlines have instituted a training program known as Cockpit Resource Management (CRM), which insures that during unexpected circumstances someone in the cockpit remains singularly focused on the most important task — flying the plane.

Cockpit Resource Management procedures are applicable to any management or entrepreneurial process. When it comes to managing the details of our lives and careers, if we don't keep our eye on the most important matters, we will get lost in the details. And often, whatever it is we are driving crashes.

The goal of strategic "dashboarding" is to provide quick, up-to-date, easy-to-read monitoring of your key performance indicators. Theoretically, dashboards enable business leaders who are bombarded with data to focus on a relatively few numbers that really matter. As a result, they can monitor long and short-term performance, quickly recognize potential problems, and identify the source of positive and negative Momentum changes. There are three principles of dashboard design and use that can be applied to any goal-oriented process.

1. Design Is the Real Trick.

The easy part is finding an extraordinary amount of data that can be tracked. The hard part is deciding which data to track and how to display it on the dashboard. In other words, what are the key indicators that measure real progress and Momentum in your particular industry or project? In some it might be new contacts, the number of repeat customers, or some other measure of relationship significance. It could even be something as obscure as the number of cups of coffee with A and B level prospects. Whatever you assign to be front-and-center on your dashboard, choose carefully. A good friend of mine calls it "items closest to the money." How you measure and monitor Momentum will indirectly determine which way you move.

2. One Dashboard Never Fits All.

It is important to recognize that for every product, project, or purpose, the front and center gauges are different. That is why one dashboard never fits all. The nature, size, and maturity of your business determine which gauges are most important and most prominent. In my days of disorganization, I spent so much time monitoring the progress of secondary issues, that it distracted me from focusing on far more critical issues.

My friend, Steve Murrell, is the founder and pastor of a 60,000-member church in Manila who rarely thinks about or counts attendance. And he certainly has never worried about it. Because of his particular philosophy of ministry, small group discipleship, attendance has little to do with his picture of success. There are people who actually count those who attended one of the eighty worship services that meet in eighteen locations throughout Metro Manila each weekend. But the leadership team rarely looks at those numbers. There are only three indicators on their dashboard — the number of small groups, the number of small group leaders completing the training course, and the number of baptisms. Steve and his team realized early on that those were the numbers that measured the true health and progress of the church. They work tirelessly to improve those numbers, but don't get distracted with less important data.

3. There Is a Time and Place for Every Indicator.

The goal of dashboarding is not to eliminate or ignore data that relates to your business plan or its progress. Gauges are arranged on a dashboard according to how frequently they need to be monitored. That doesn't mean an obscure indicator is not critically important. For instance, the oil and temperature gauges on your car measure the two most important fluid levels. If those indicators get into the red, you will ruin the engine in only a few miles. But the speedometer is the most prominent. The reason is that oil and coolant levels rarely vary, while speed is a critical measurement that varies constantly. There are some key indicators that you need to monitor constantly, some gauges you check periodically, and some that represent progress you need to review at particular milestones during the year or during your lifetime.

What's on your dashboard? The best business development plans will not work without systematic habits, follow through, and proper monitoring. Developing your own customized dashboard in some form is essential to monitoring the Momentum of your business, career, and even personal life. It enables you to focus on the most important thing when and only when it becomes the most important thing. If you are trying to focus on everything at once, you are never able to truly focus on anything. Without focus, it is impossible to accrue Relationship Momentum in its purest form.

6
L'AUDACE

"Audacity, Audacity, Always Audacity!"
— Frederick the Great

Throughout my years in the trenches of innovation and business development, I have found that there are a few key attributes that enable people to be successful with their ideas. I've also seen products, projects, and entities (some of my own) fail, due to a few missing ingredients in the recipe. The general principle, the "big idea" of this book is Relationship Momentum, and it is expressed by a formula:

$$Rm = E^3 V_s$$
Relationship Momentum is (Brand, Value, and Ambassador Equity)
Multiplied by (Strategic Velocity)

Simple definitions:

> *Relationship Momentum* is the art and science of activating ideas through the accumulation of Brand, Value, and Ambassador Equity, creating relational movement in a consistent and strategic direction.

> *Brand Equity* is how people perceive you and in contrast to (or congruence with) who you truly are.

> *Value Equity* is your gift to the world. It is the needs you meet and the difference you make.

> *Ambassador Equity* is your ability to influence the world through others who are equipped and dedicated to telling your story.

> *Strategic Velocity* is your deliberate (strategic) movement in a consistent direction.

In the beginning of this book I talked about creating movement in a consistent direction and combining it with a measure of audacity. The trouble with high audacity is that it often leads to high presumption. Boldly thinking that we can do all things sometimes leads us to blindly charge ahead, without thinking at all. There must be an element of pause in the passion.

One of my former mentors used to talk about "meek audacity." At first it seemed like an oxymoron. Moses, who led the entire nation of Israel out of bondage from the Egyptian Pharaohs, was said to be, "very meek, above all the men which were upon the face of the earth" (Numbers 12:3). The great leader-deliverer, the meekest man on earth... is that another oxymoron? Not really. It is rather a misunderstanding of the meaning of meekness.

I like to think of meekness as audacity under control, or bridled audacity. In the days before the mechanization of warfare, horses that were trained for war were a powerful and terrifying force on the battlefield. They were commonly referred to as Meek Horses. Only those with a certain temperament could be trained as such horses. They had to be ferocious to the point of trampling the enemy combatants under foot, yet calm, submissive to their master, and under control in the midst of deafening canon fire. When I think of a Meek Horse, I think of this passage in Job; "He paws fiercely rejoicing in his strength, and charges into the fray. He laughs at fear, afraid of nothing; he does not shy away from the sword." We should aim to have this kind of discipline and fierceness in our endeavors.

Frederick the Great

Napoleon considered Frederick William II of Prussia to be the greatest military genius in history. Frederick was known as a master tactician on the battlefield, as well as for his bravery. Because he insisted on staying close to the front line, Frederick is said to have had six horses shot out from under him. He was perhaps best known for his valiant stand against a coalition of Austria, France, Russia, Saxony, and Sweden in the 1760s. Frederick, who came to be known as Frederick the Great, was once quoted as saying, *"L'audace, L'audace, Tejours, L'audace!"* Translation: "Audacity, Audacity, Always Audacity!"

Audacity is exactly what one needs when setting off on a journey fraught with danger and turmoil — perhaps not physical danger, but indeed the danger of failure, embarrassment, opposition, and great loss. Notwithstanding the danger, many of us can hardly restrain ourselves from launching into that great new product, project, or purpose. Visionaries are not easily managed or restrained. Accountability and strategy are what restrains this unbridled enthusiasm. Accountability is usually (but not always) to a person. Strategic accountability is usually to a predetermined plan that limits the extent to which we wander off track. One of those key ingredients I mentioned at the beginning will come in very handy. What we need is some of that "bridled audacity."

How Do We Get There?

In these pages we have discussed a formula for making ideas move. We have compared and dissected positive and negative examples of Relationship Momentum. Examples of companies that have been able to create and profit from positive Momentum (Microsoft, Apple, and Under Armour). Examples of visionary causes (the Civil Rights Movement, the Arab Spring, and Every Nation Ministries). Examples of products (Converse Chuck Taylors, and FUBU Gear). We even discussed a few negative examples such as British Petroleum and Groupon.

There is a lot to learn from these industry giants. There is also much to learn from the people and companies that create their products, projects, and purposes in your local markets. Which ones succeed? Which ones fail? One thing of which I have become convinced — you can tie those successes and failures to Relationship Momentum.

The idea here is not to simply emulate these examples but to learn some of the underlying principles from them for your own journey. The only thing you can do today is to commit to making Relationship Momentum your focus. Elect your target and then find your True North, your picture of success. Take inventory and continue on the path by setting specific goals that will help you build Relationship Momentum.

Use the brain tree below to design your path. As driven people, we have a desire to make progress on a daily basis. The desired track is simple, make your Equities grow. I want to encourage you to begin somewhere, anywhere. Make sure to document your strategy and your progress. Combine your bridled audacity with strategy and accountability. Then watch your Equities multiply before your eyes.

7
THE BIG WIN
THE PURPOSEFUL WEEK

"Winning is a habit. Unfortunately, so is losing."
— Vince Lombardi

Someone once asked me what my perfect week would look like. That's a fun thing to consider. If there were such a thing as a perfect week, I would spend part of it with family and friends at a beach somewhere, followed by a few rounds of golf with my son and father. We all would shoot blazing 59s, which would be a remarkable score for any golfer, but miraculous for my son since he is only three years old. But since I was asked — that's my perfect week.

But I'm not fantasizing about a perfect week that would require every imaginable circumstance falling into the proper order, something that might happen only once in a lifetime. I would set my sights, not on something that I was waiting to happen to me, but on the kind of week that I could create and even maintain. I am much more interested in a purposeful week that could be repeated with great regularity.

Purposeful days and weeks are those on which I feel that I have accomplished something of strategic significance — that is, I have moved the ball down the field toward my goals. I found that the most consistent way to move my ideas and initiatives is by organizing my time and priorities around the concept and the formula for Relationship Momentum. To be more specific, the repeatable, purposeful week would include forward movement toward building and maintaining the Three Equities (Brand, Value, and Ambassador). It would also include personal growth in the three spheres (Spiritual, Personal, and Vocational). Often weekly advances toward such big objectives are measured in micro-movement, but it is consistently forward movement nonetheless.

Consistent movement is important. In terms of Momentum, you know how much energy it takes to get something moving from a standing-still position. Remember Newton's First Law — objects standing still (at rest) tend to stay that way unless an outside force is exerted upon them. When friction and Drag are taken into consideration, it takes a lot more energy to get an object (or a project) moving than it does to keep them moving. In the real world of projects, causes, and personal relationships, have you ever ignored one of those for a few weeks, a few months, or even a few years, only to realize how difficult it is to regain Momentum?

I began trying to form purposeful weeks out of daily habits, with the Relationship Momentum concepts and the Relationship Momentum Equation at the forefront of my mind. It was a bit awkward at times, and overwhelming at others. However, I eventually began to figure out the order of Momentum in my personal life and business. That revelation about the unique self doesn't come over night and it doesn't suddenly appear when you finally realize you need it. It emerges from a process of identifying your sources of Momentum, Drag, Potential Energy, etc. When you do get into that groove, it can actually be quite liberating and empowering.

Planning Your Week

I do not attempt to program my whole year in advance. There are too many tactical responses (or in sailing terms, "tacks") that I need to take in order to navigate the most efficient course to my strategic objective. In other words, I have found that for me, overscheduling without flexibility is a Momentum killer. This self-knowledge is something I discovered by continually evaluating my forward progress and analyzing the sources of positive or negative Relationship Momentum.

What I originally thought to be overwhelming, if not impossible, I eventually found to be quite possible, when all of the Equities and Spheres of Relationship Momentum consistently move in a positive direction. It doesn't mean a win at every single challenge on every single day. That's not the point. It is just a matter of a belief, trust, confidence, and the sense of progress. I know that if I efficiently employ Relationship Momentum in my life and in my ideas, it will always tend to propel me forward.

I begin my day by looking at the equation, $Rm= E^3V_s$. Then I spend a few moments visualizing the True North, the picture of success, of winning. I contemplate the potential distractions, the key relationships, my Brand, Value, and Ambassador Equities. I think about that picture in terms of priorities. Does my picture of success in life and my purposeful week sync with my fundamental priorities — the three spheres (Spiritual, Personal, and Vocational)? We cannot underestimate the interconnectivity of the three Spheres. Balance all three, and it can create a lot of positive Momentum in your life. Allow them to go off-kilter, and everything can come crashing down around you.

Scoring Your Week

As important as it is to plan your week, it is imperative to keep score. If you are losing (not gaining Momentum), you need to know it. If you are winning, you need to celebrate it and hardwire the habit. Colin Powell said it best when he explained that, "Perpetual Optimism is a Force Multiplier!" Momentum begets Momentum and we need to be encouraged by our progress.

Scoring your week is simple. There are Three Equities. Simply put, your E^3 needs to gain scale weekly in order to create Relationship Momentum for your products, projects or purpose. Please use the scorecard below as a guide for tracking your progress. You do not need extravagant software or web applications to get moving in the right direction. The heavier your ideas are and the greater your velocity, the more sophisticated you may have to become, but remember this, Momentum begets Momentum and you have to start somewhere.

– RM Scorecard –
$Rm=E^3Vs$

- **True North:** Did you move towards the Goal?
- **Weekly Plan:** Did you take time to be Strategic?
- **Brand Equity:** Emblem, Ethos, Elevator, Evolve
- **Value Equity:** Real, Relevant, Transferrable, Escalate
- **Ambassador Equity:** Business Ambassadors, Embassy of Commerce, Power of the Crowd (Social Media), Ambassador Councils

Momentum Meter
- 90-100 - Optimum Momentum Week
- 80-90 - Gaining Momentum
- 60-80 - Positive Movement
- 40-60 - Stagnant
- 20-40 - Contracting
- 0-20 - Vortex

Scoring Scale
- 15-20 - Gaining Momentum
- 10-15 - Maintaining
- 5-10 - Losing Ground
- 1-5 - Kidding Yourself

Total **Rm** Score:

RELATIONSHIP MOMENTUM

Only the Beginning
The secret to making our ideas and initiatives progress is found in the quantity and quality of our relationships as they relate to our ideas.

As important as the experience you create for your relationships, your own experience is imperative for a successful journey. We have an innate drive in us to see progress. We need to win! This cerebral power of confidence provides movement within us and our sphere and is as important to our ideas as anything.

If you are taking the time to be strategic and deliberate, if you are accumulating weight behind your Brand, Value, and Ambassador Equities on a weekly basis, you are almost guaranteed to win. If you focus on these concepts and apply them persistently, it won't be long before you see the power of Relationship Momentum beginning to work in your favor, and you will most certainly see your ideas and your endeavors move!

ACKNOWLEDGEMENTS

This book was a two year project on the heels of a seven year journey. I have been in search of answers for myself, my colleagues and anyone who has ever had the courage to engage the inventive process. Without the grace of God and the inspiration that only comes from He who is the author of all ideas, this manuscript would not have been a possibility. I am thankful to all of those who have aided me on my mission. I am happy to say that the wind in my sails is not my own and that this is only the beginning!

So many people need to be thanked for their encouragement, constructive criticism, intellectual property, and assistance. I want to thank my wife Kimberly for her love and her consistent message that I am her King. My son, Brian Timothy Church II for inspiring me to be a man that is worthy of such a gift as being his father. My father for being a real man, for his teachings and for raising me to have an entrepreneurial spirit. My mother for her prayers, ideas, and foresight. She never gave up on me. My family has walked with me through this endeavor and I appreciate their authentic belief behind my initiatives.

I want to thank Walter Walker. Walt has been my writing partner, coach, and collaborator. I can honestly say that you are reading a completed and significant product because of the work and advice from this man. I am glad that God gave me a concept that Walter finally could get excited about!

I would like to thank David Dalton, who has been there with me from the beginning. David challenged me to read my own writings, follow my own advice and to develop Momentum for my own cause. David's ideas, stories, and feedback helped to mold the manuscript you are reading today.

When attempting to combine concepts in business, relationships, and physics, one should not make the journey alone. I want to thank Dr. Brian Miller and Dr. Ming Wang for their guidance, encouragement, and friendship.

Thank you to my Publishers, David Dunham and Joel Dunham, for their friendship and for taking a chance on me. George Shinn, Bill Bailey, Rick Myers, Robert Deloach, and the Men of Aslan for helping much more than they would give themselves credit for.

The creative process is a tough one. I now have an even deeper level of respect for those who dare to dream, innovate, and create in the face of life's obstacles. I am appreciative of the people who have been an encouragement to me and my dreams. May God bless you in all of your endeavors!

CPSIA information can be obtained at www.ICGtesting.com
Printed in the USA
LVOW06*0800160813

348153LV00001B/2/P